Amedeo Clemente Modigliani

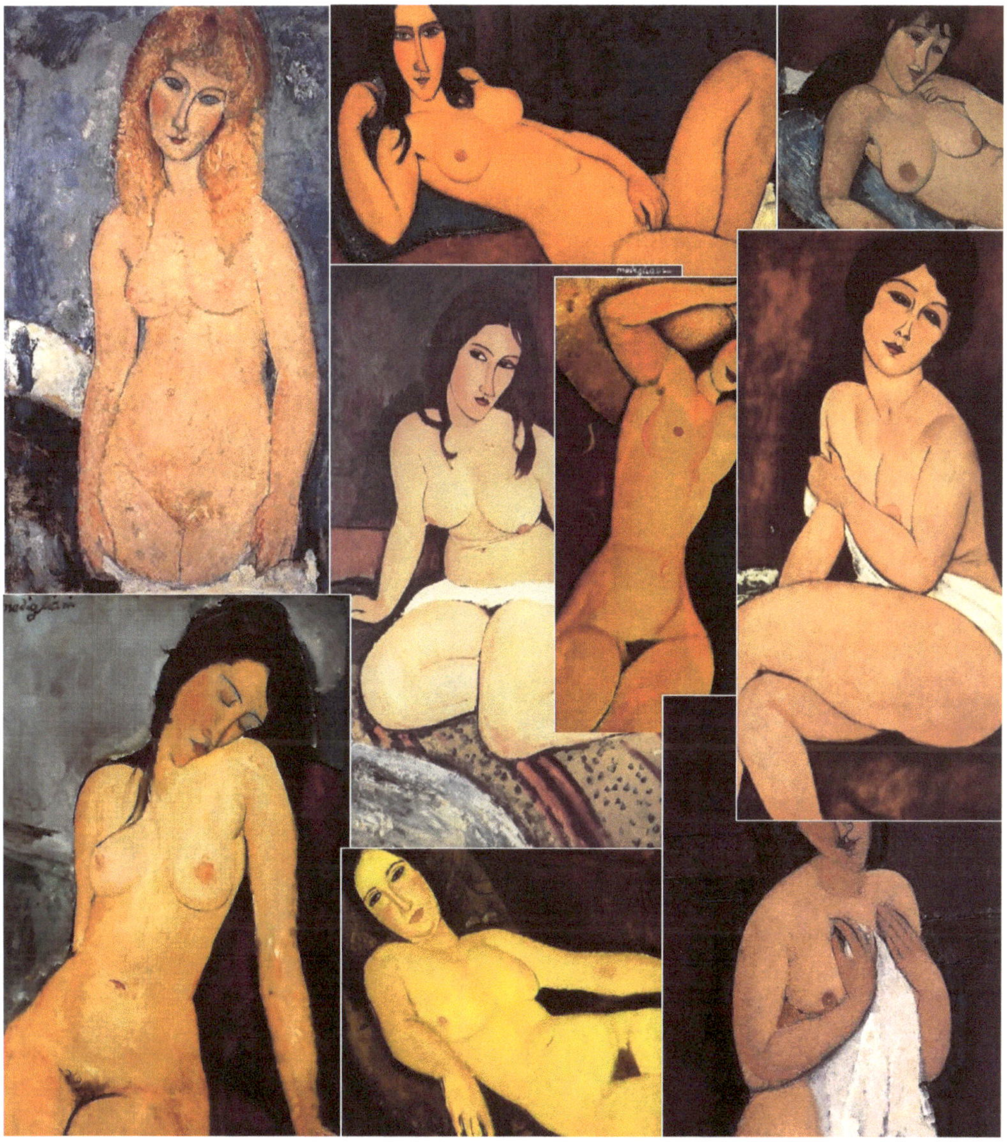

Edited by Lacey Belinda Smith

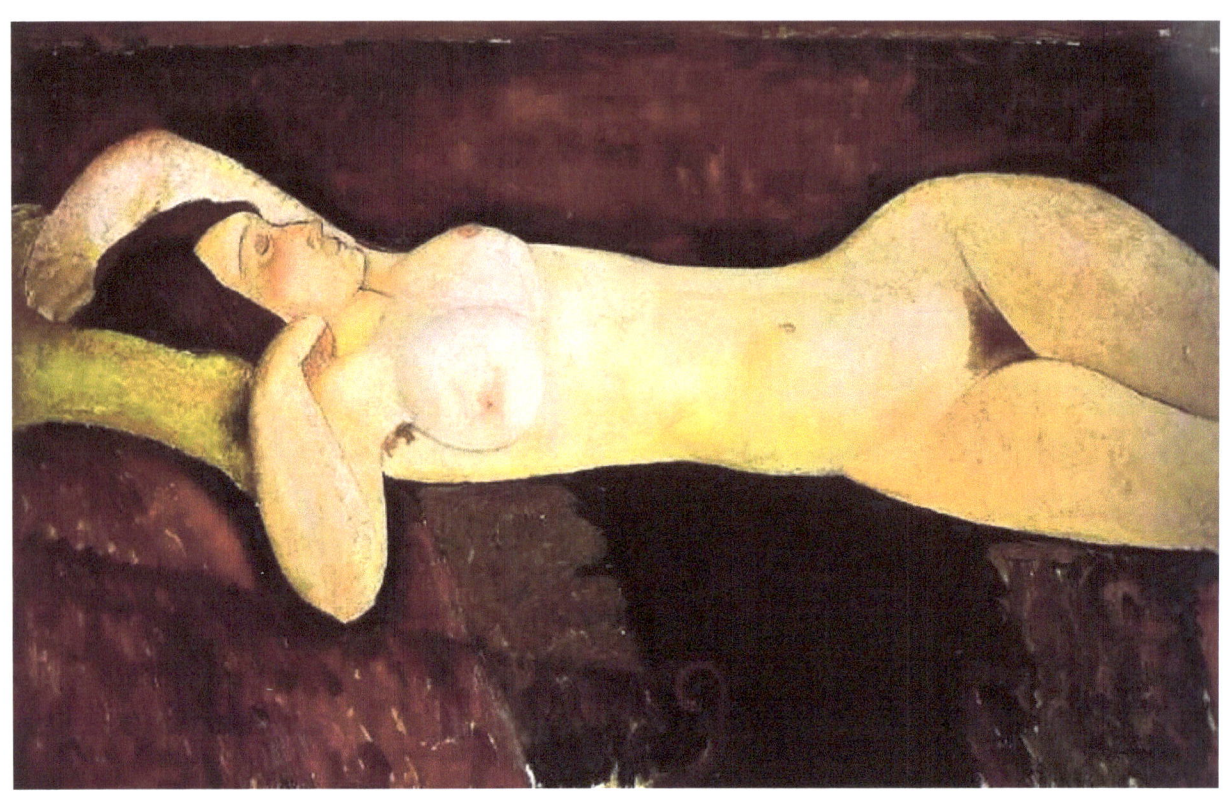

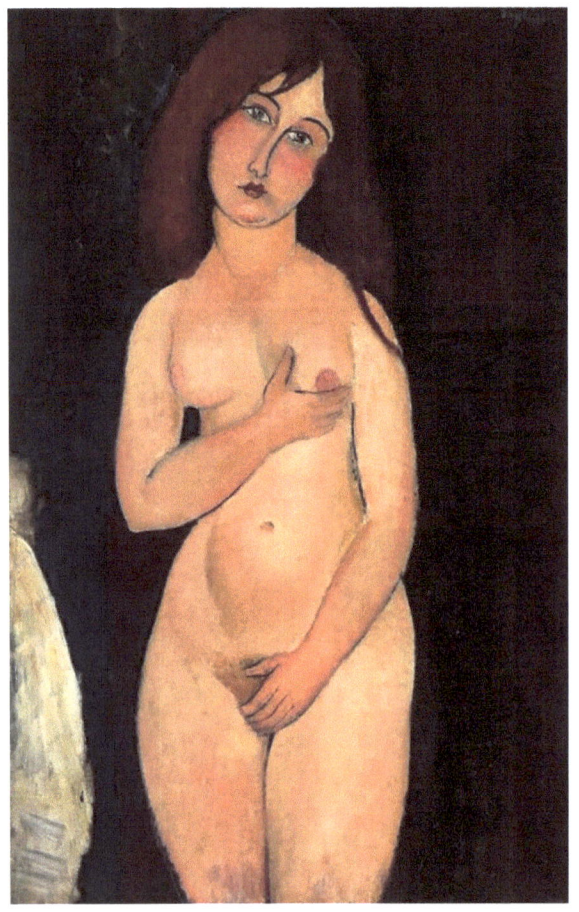

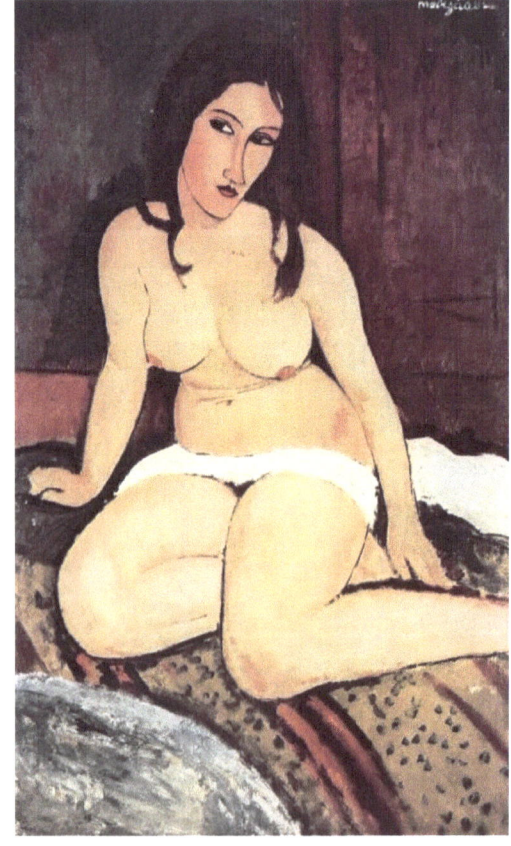

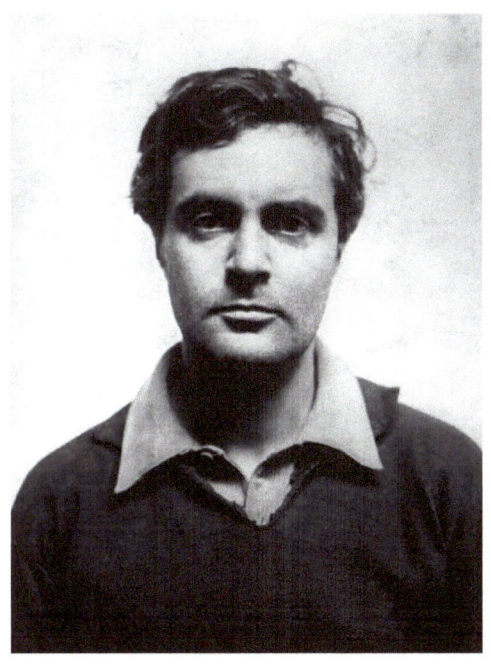 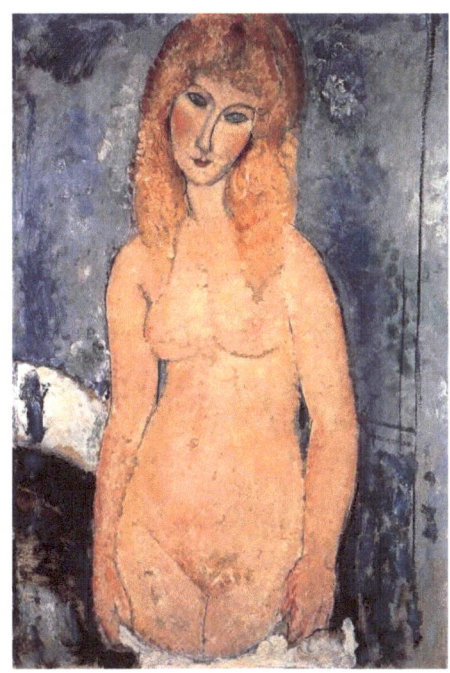

Amedeo Clemente Modigliani (July 12, 1884 - January 24, 1920)

Amedeo Modigliani was a Jewish Italian modern artist. His father was in the money-changing business; but when the business went bankrupt, the family lived in poverty. He was a painter and sculptor known for his simplified and elongated forms.

Amedeo Modigliani was on born July 12, 1884 in Livorno, Italy. After studying in Italy, Modigliani settled in Paris and exhibited at the Salon des Indépendants where he began to create his unique style. Modigliani modernized two of the enduring themes of art history--the portrait and the nude. His style was characterized by a sense of melancholy, elongated proportions, and mask-like faces. He was influenced by such sources as Constantin Brancusi and African art.

In 1917 he began painting a series of female nudes that are among his best works. Modigliani's nudes scandalized audiences with their depiction of features such as pubic hair and their raw, brazenfaced sexuality. In 1917 Modigliani held a one-man exhibition in Paris which was closed within a few hours by the Paris Chief of Police, who considered the nudes stupefying and scandalous. These paintings were a celebration of the woman's form and sensuality. Modigliani died in 1920 of tuberculosis at age 35.

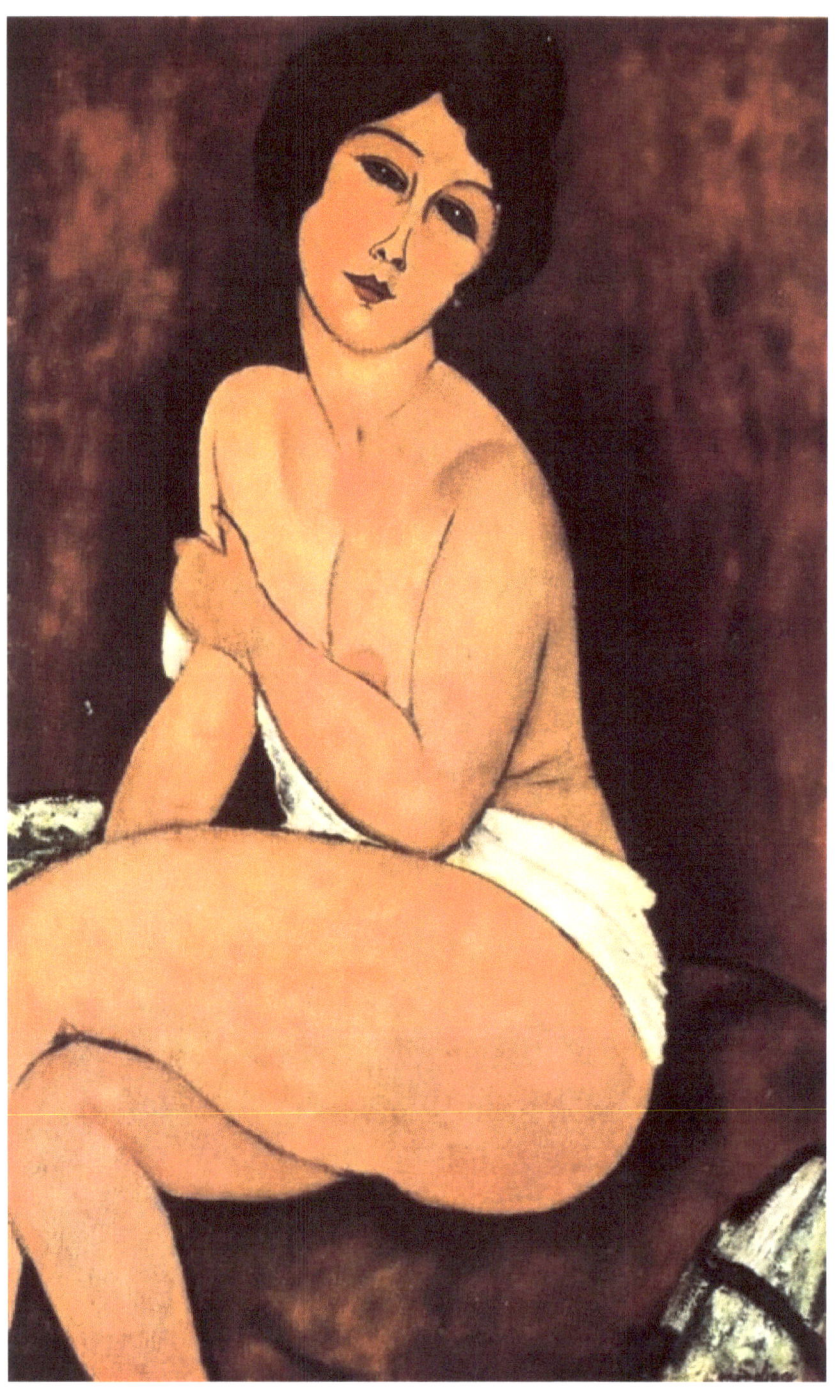

Large Seated nude, Paris, France; **Expressionism**, Private Collection

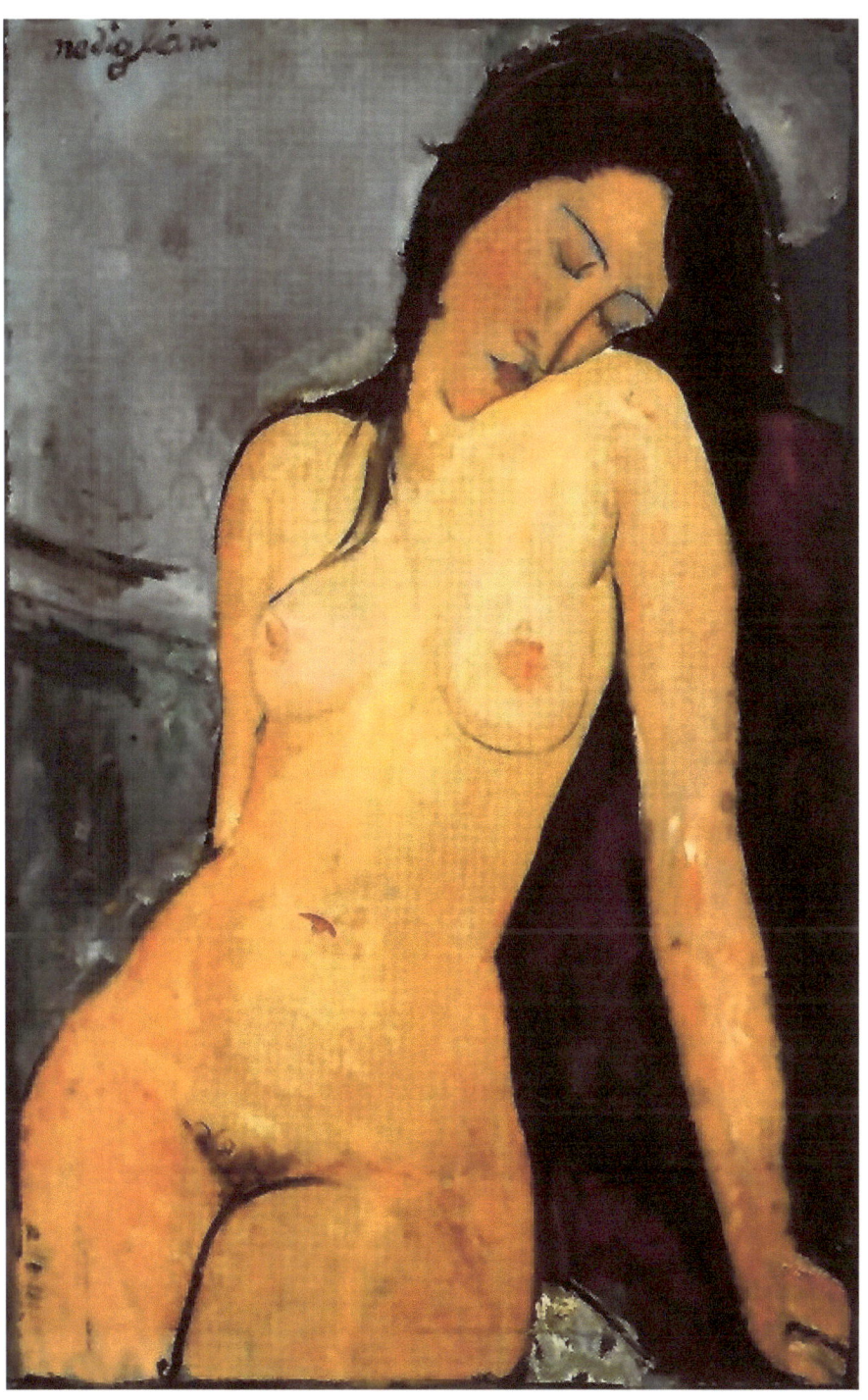

Female nude, c.1916, Paris, France; Expressionism; Courtauld Institute
of Art, London, UK

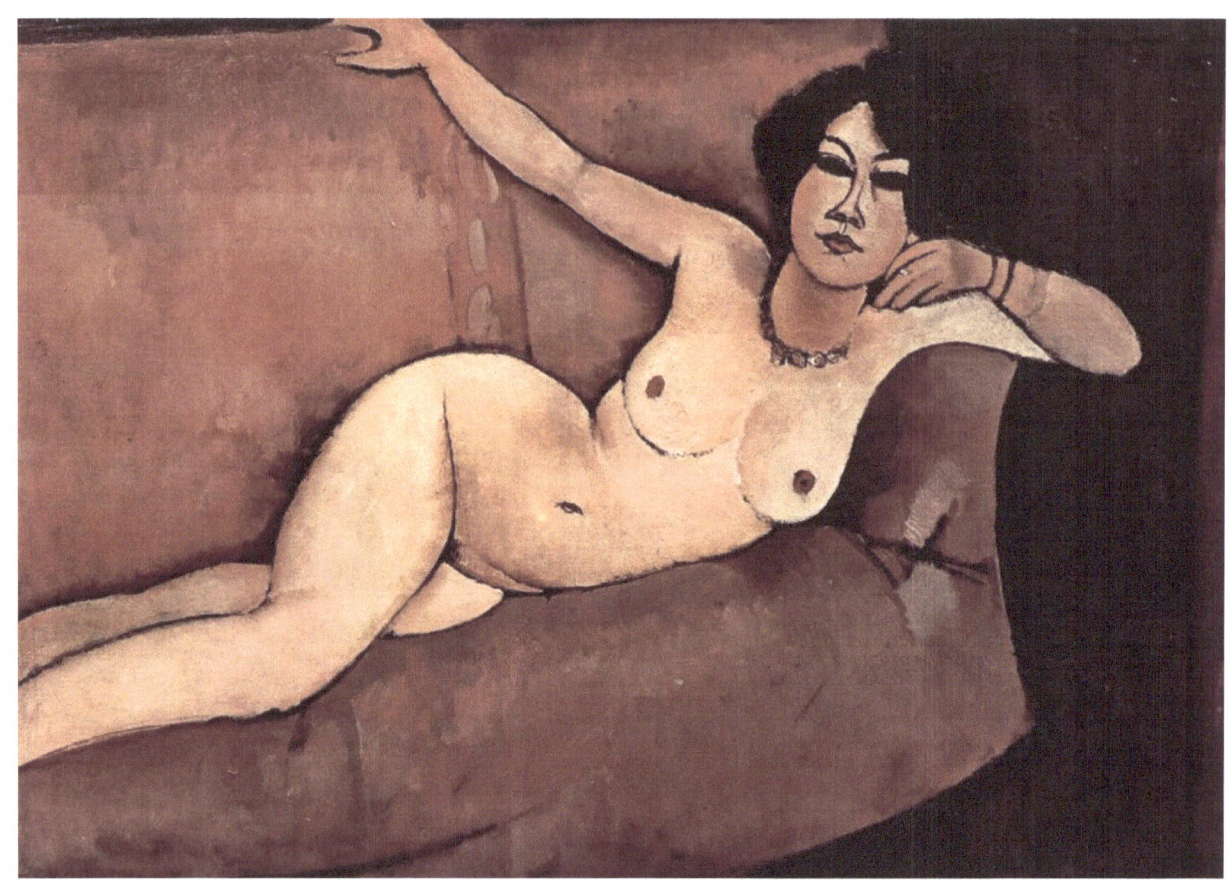

Reclining nude with Arms Folded under Her Head, 1916; Paris, France;

Expressionism; Bührle Foundation, Zürich, Switzerland

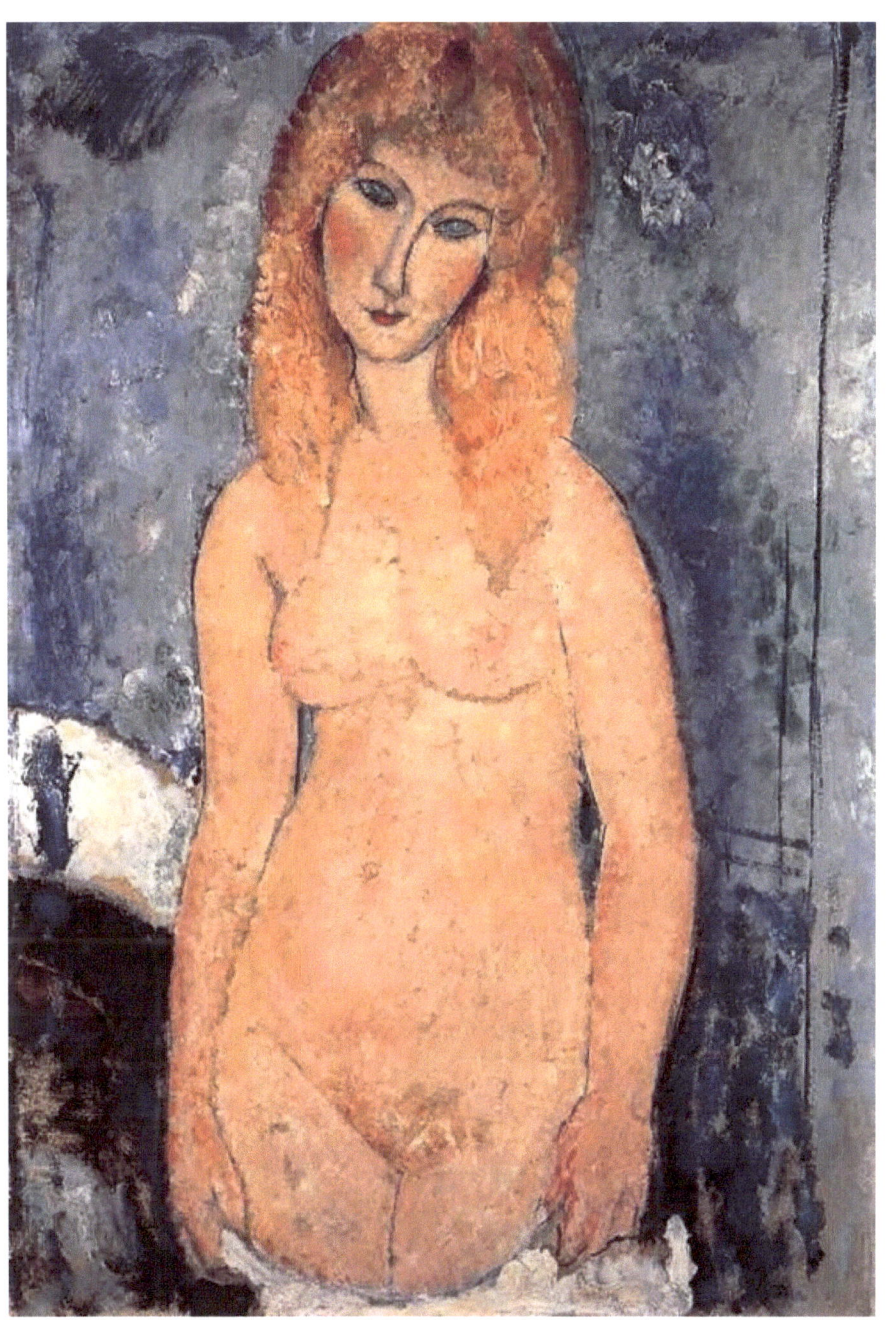

Blonde nude, 1917; Paris, France; Expressionism

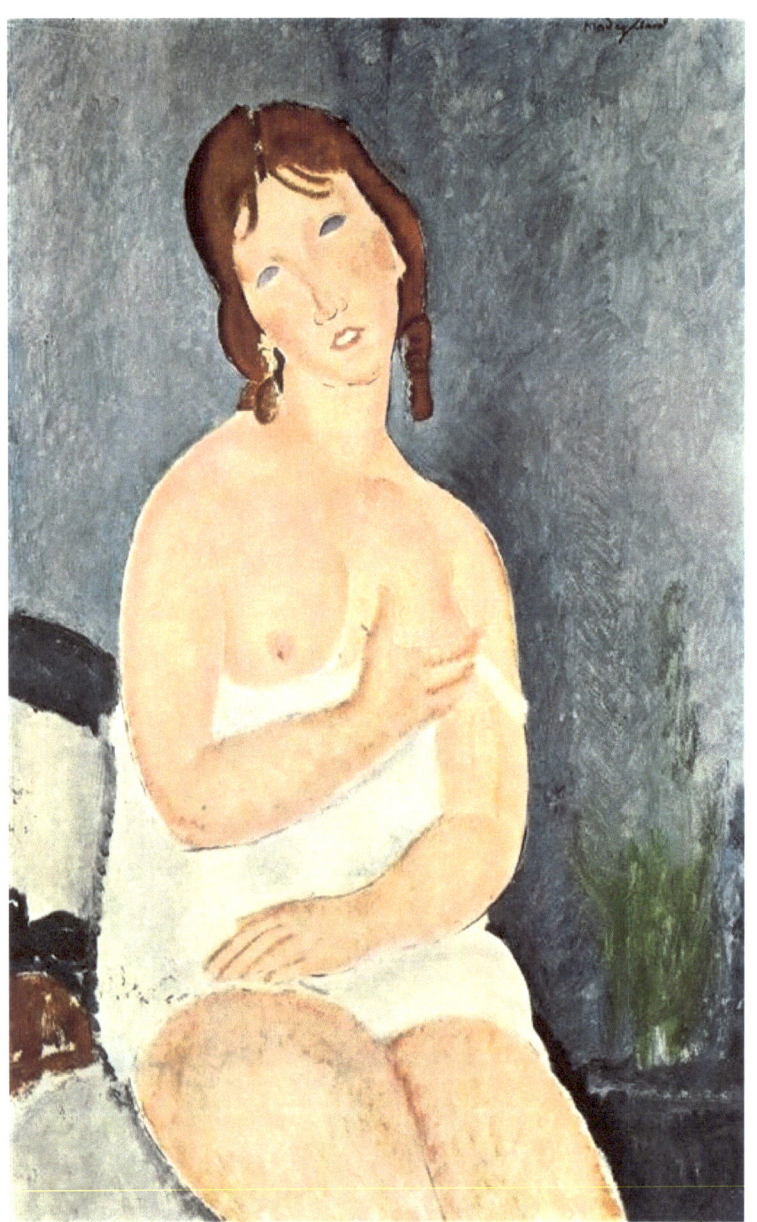

Young Woman in a Shirt (The Little Milkmaid); Paris, France;
Expressionism, Private Collection

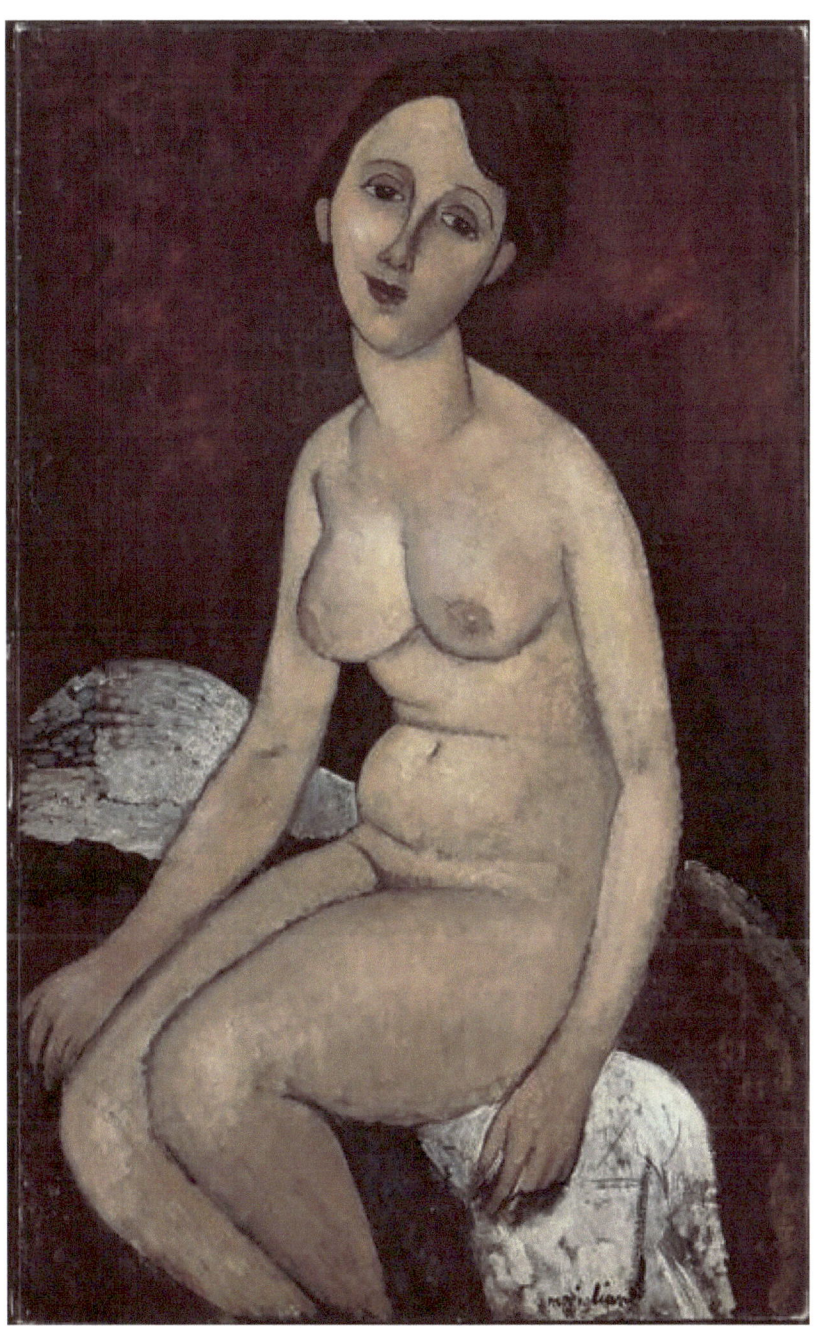

Seated nude; Paris, France; Expressionism, Musée des Beaux-Arts, Lyon, France

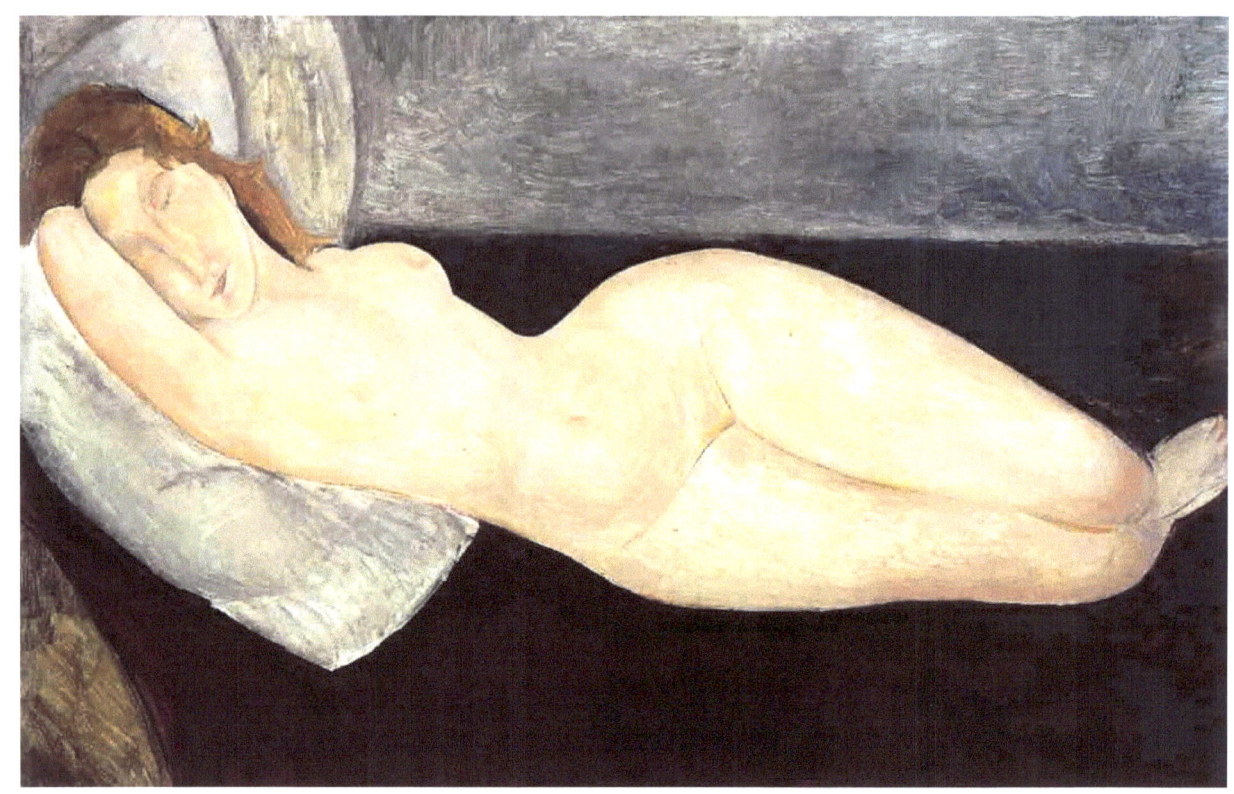

Reclining nude with head resting on right arm, 1919; Paris, France;

Expressionism; Galleria Nazionale d'Arte Moderna e Contemporanea, Rome, Italy

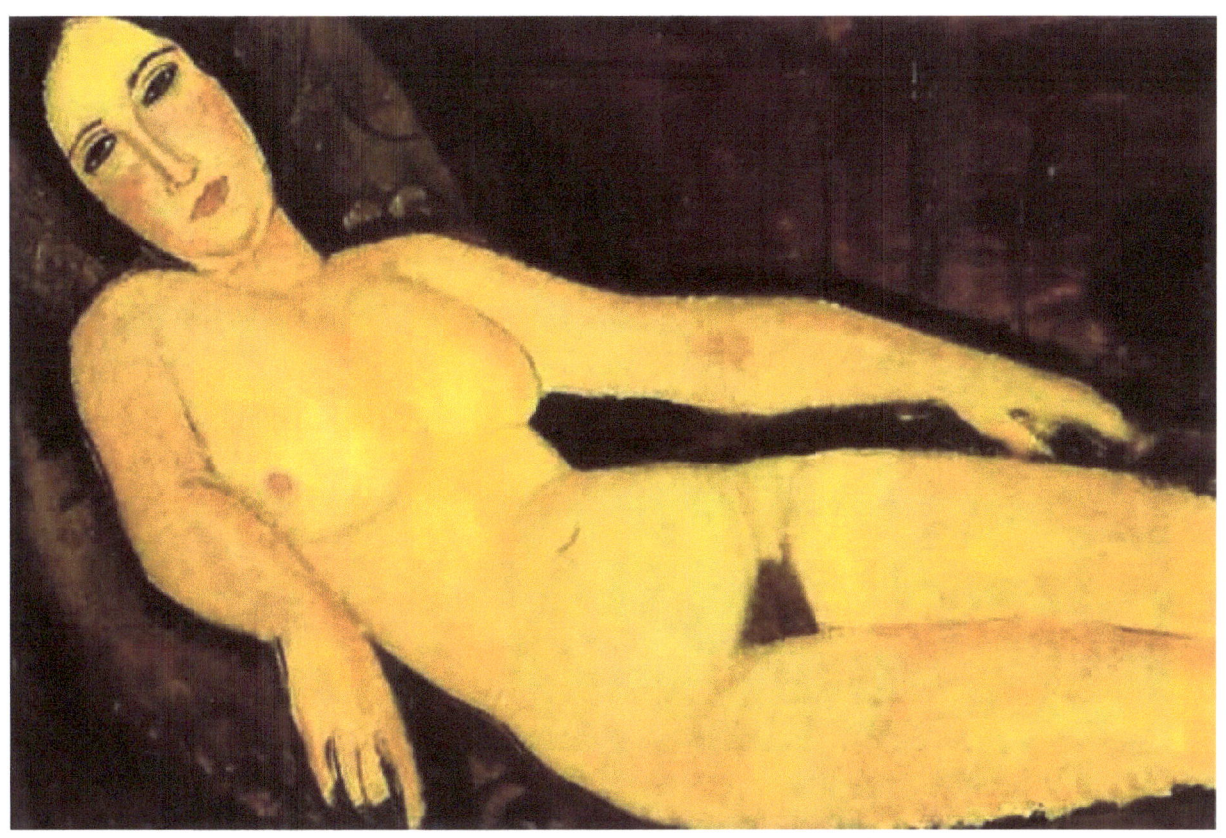

Nude on sofa, 1918; Paris, France; Expressionism, National Gallery of Art, Washingon, DC, USA

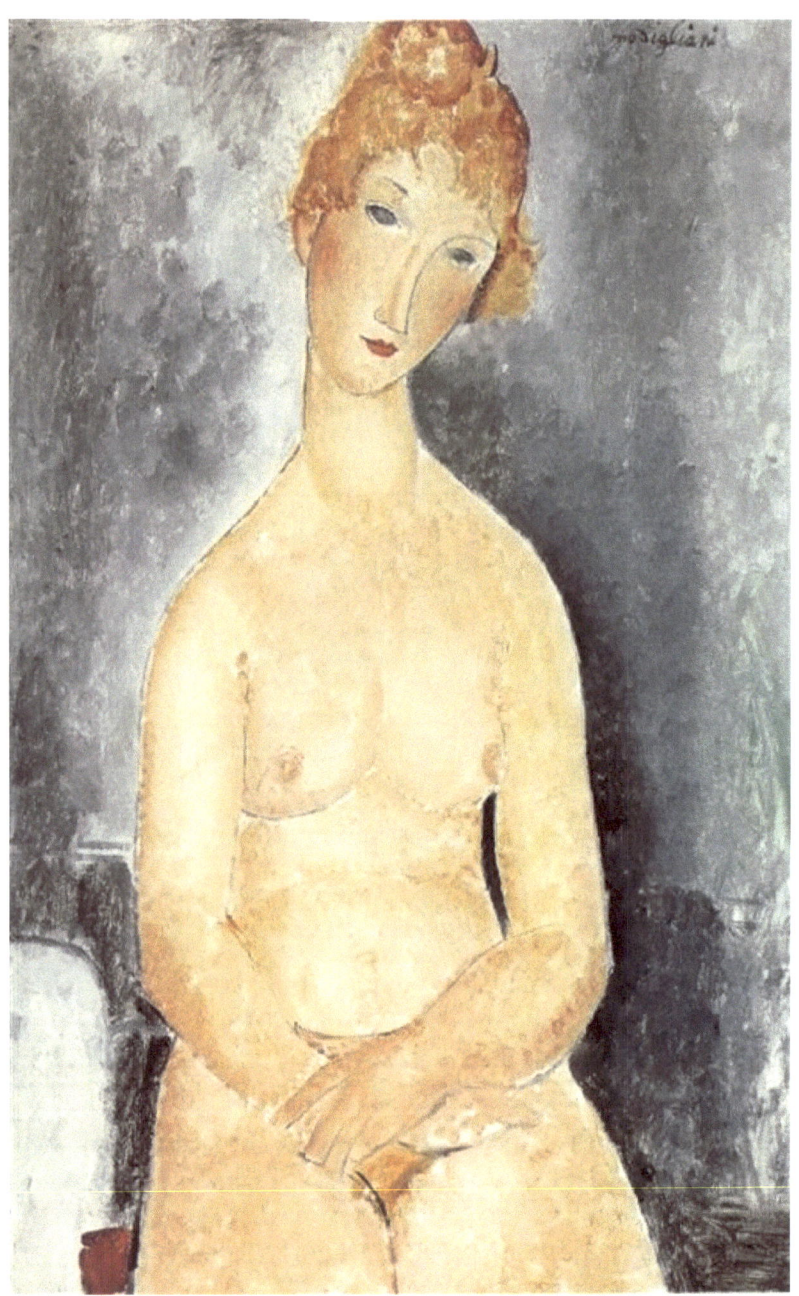

Seated nude, 1918; Paris, France; Expressionism, Private Collection

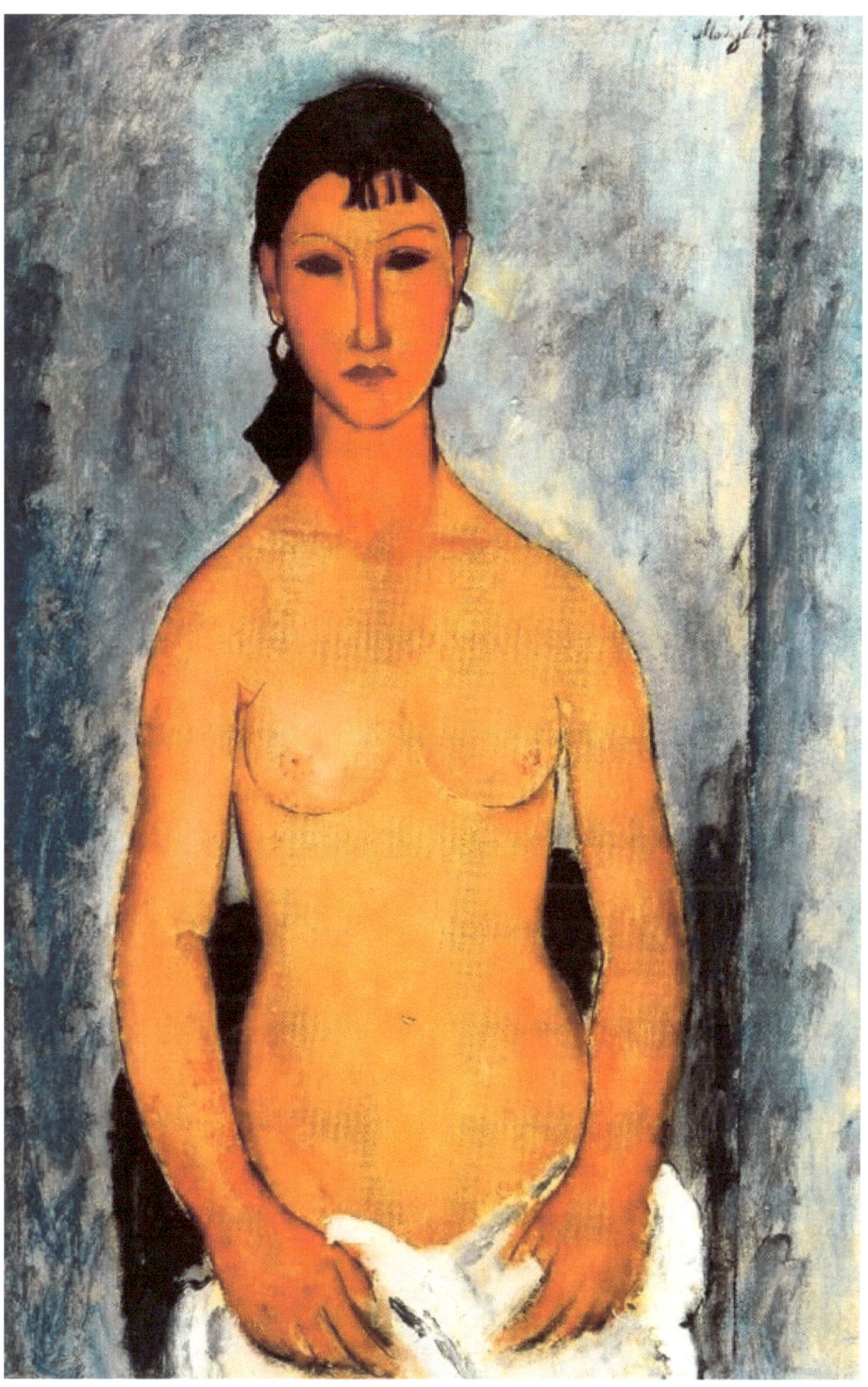

Standing nude (Elvira), 1918; Paris, France; Expressionism, Walter Hadorn collection, Bern, Switzerland

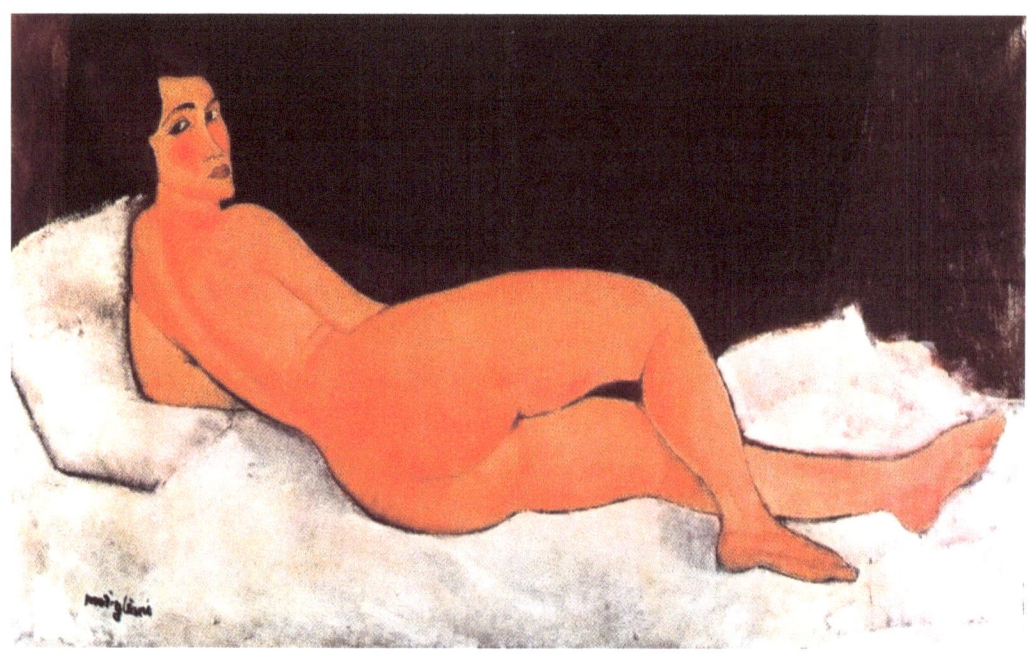

Lying nude, 1917, Paris, France; Expressionism, Private Collection

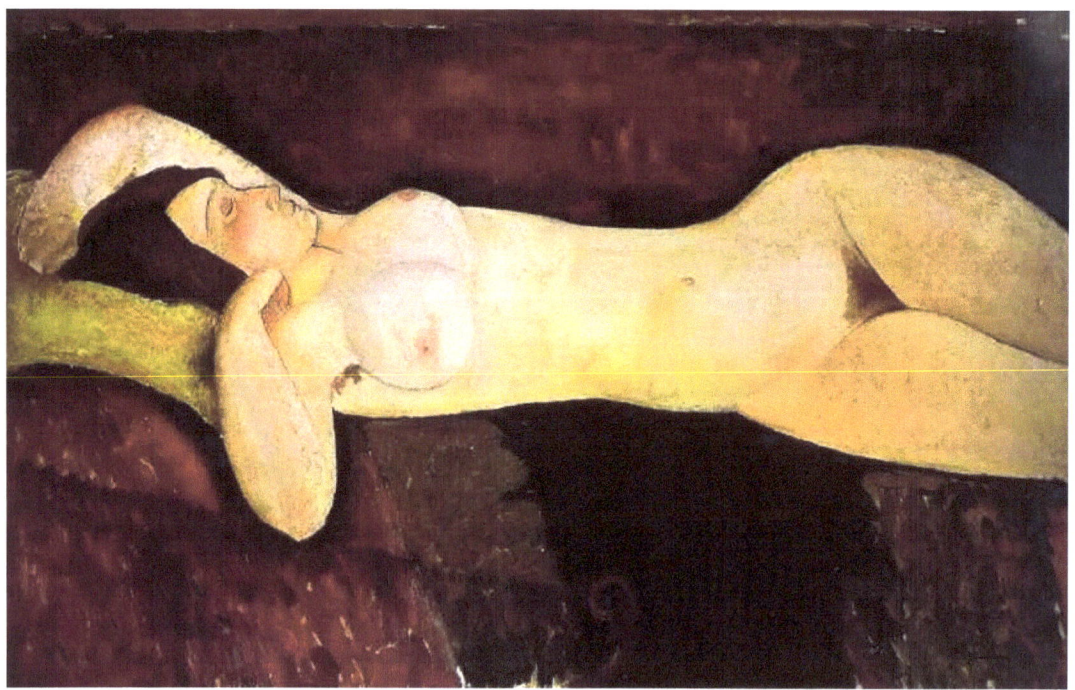

Le grand Nu (The great nude), 1917, Paris, France; Expressionism;
Museum of Modern Art, New York, USA

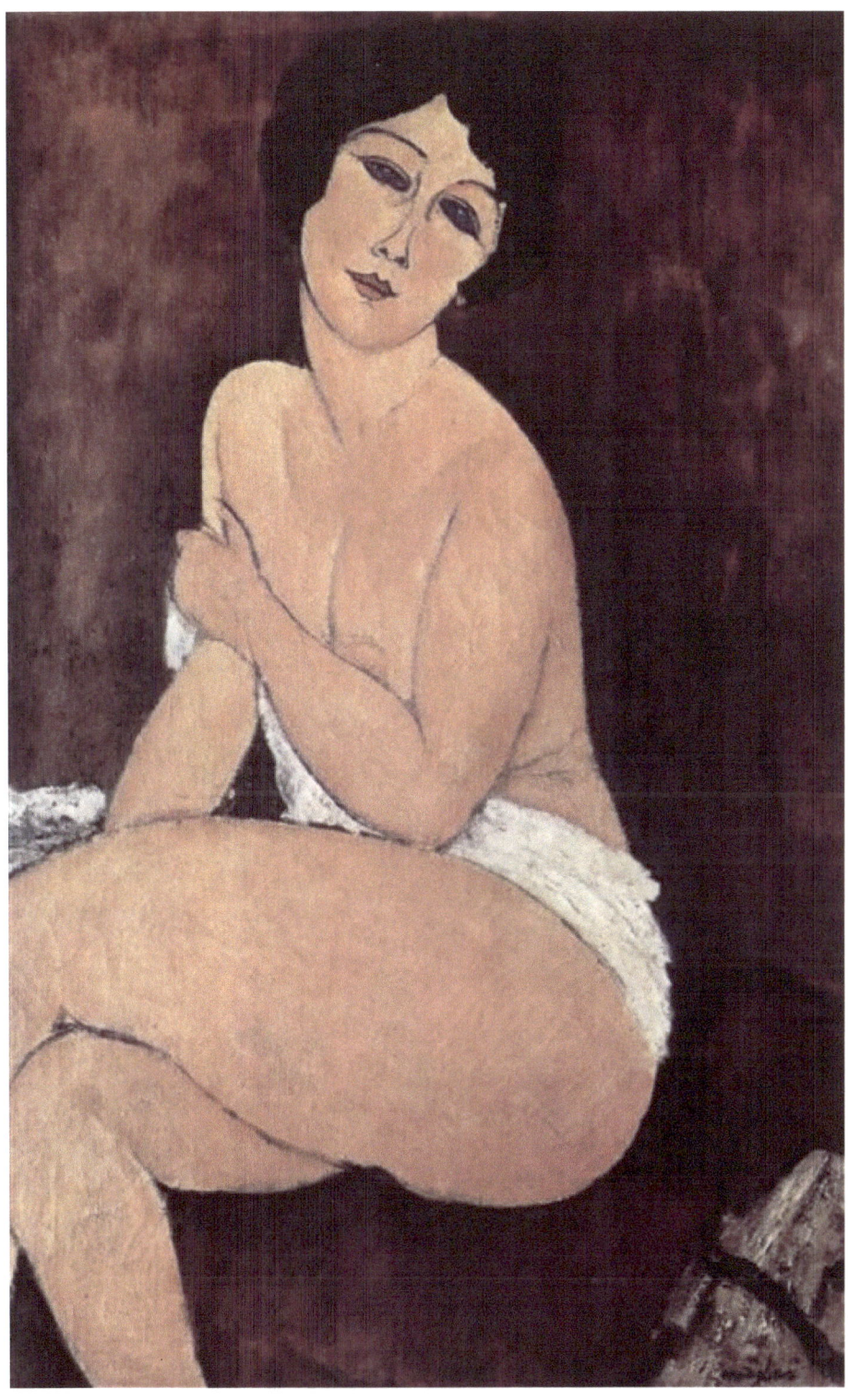

Nude seating on a sofa, **917; Paris, France, Expressionism**; **Private Collection**

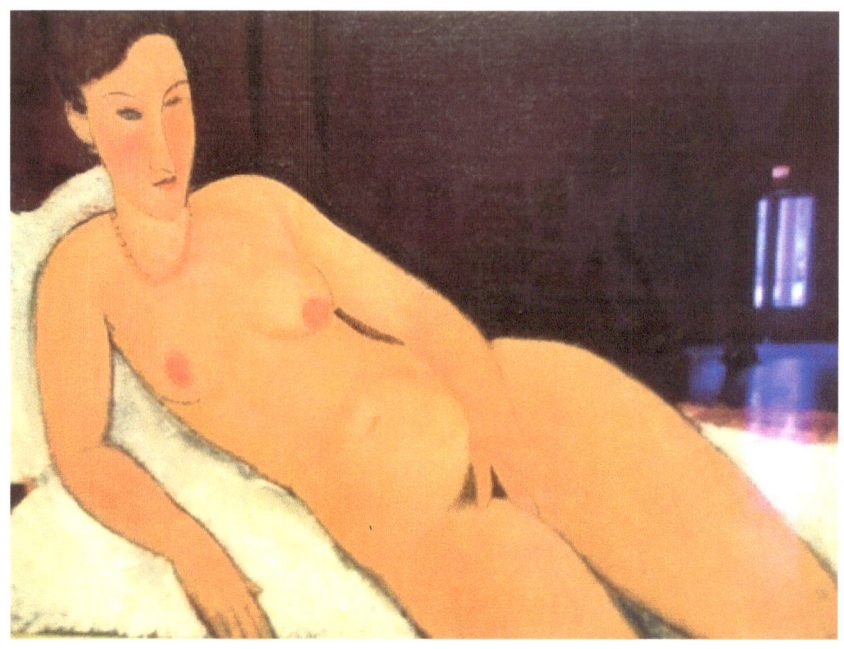

Nude with Coral Necklace, 1917; Paris, France; Expressionism; Allen Memorial Art Museum (AMAM), Oberlin, Ohio, USA

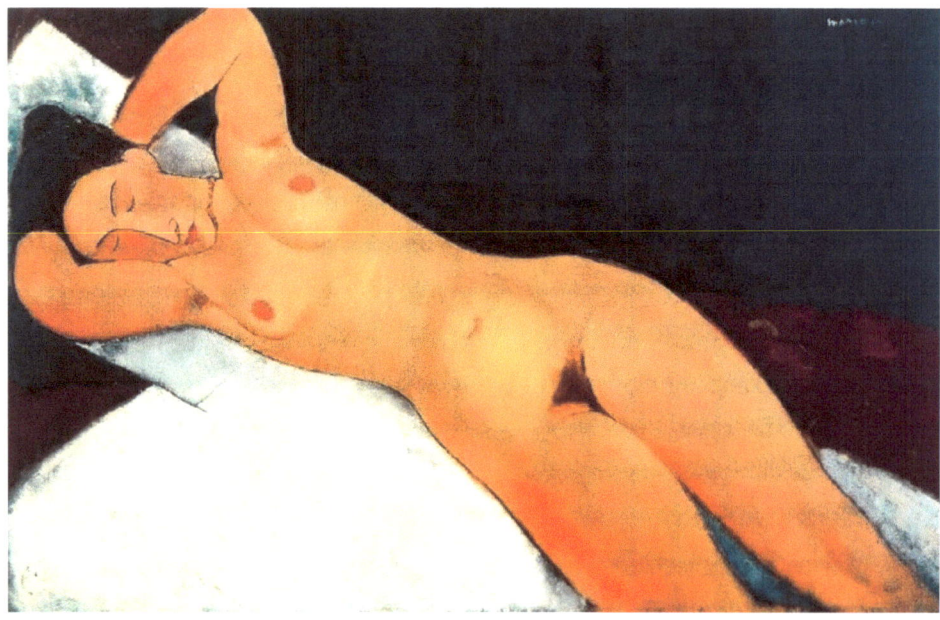

Nude with Necklace, 1917; Paris, France; Expressionism; Solomon R. Guggenheim Museum, New York, USA

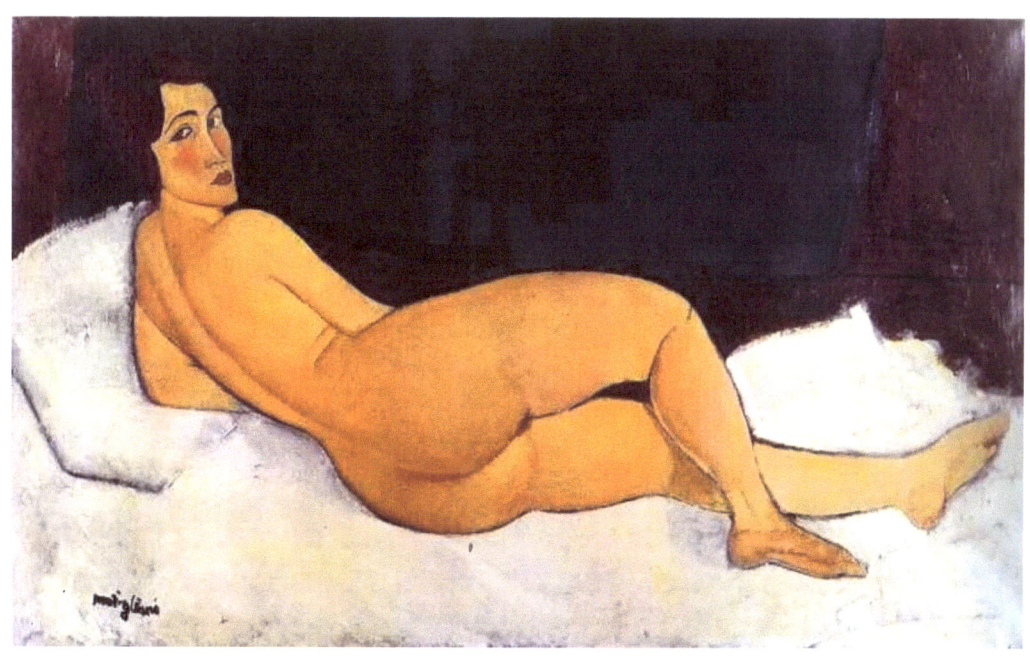

Nude Looking over Her Right Shoulder, 1917; Paris, France;
Expressionism, Private Collection

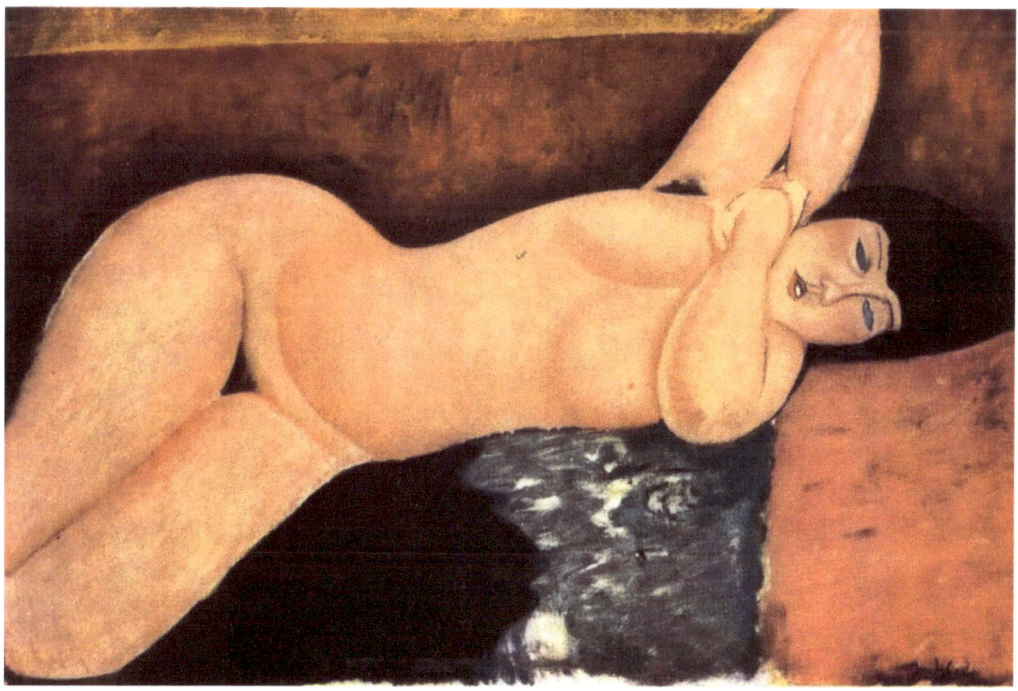

Reclining nude, c.1917; Paris, France; Expressionism

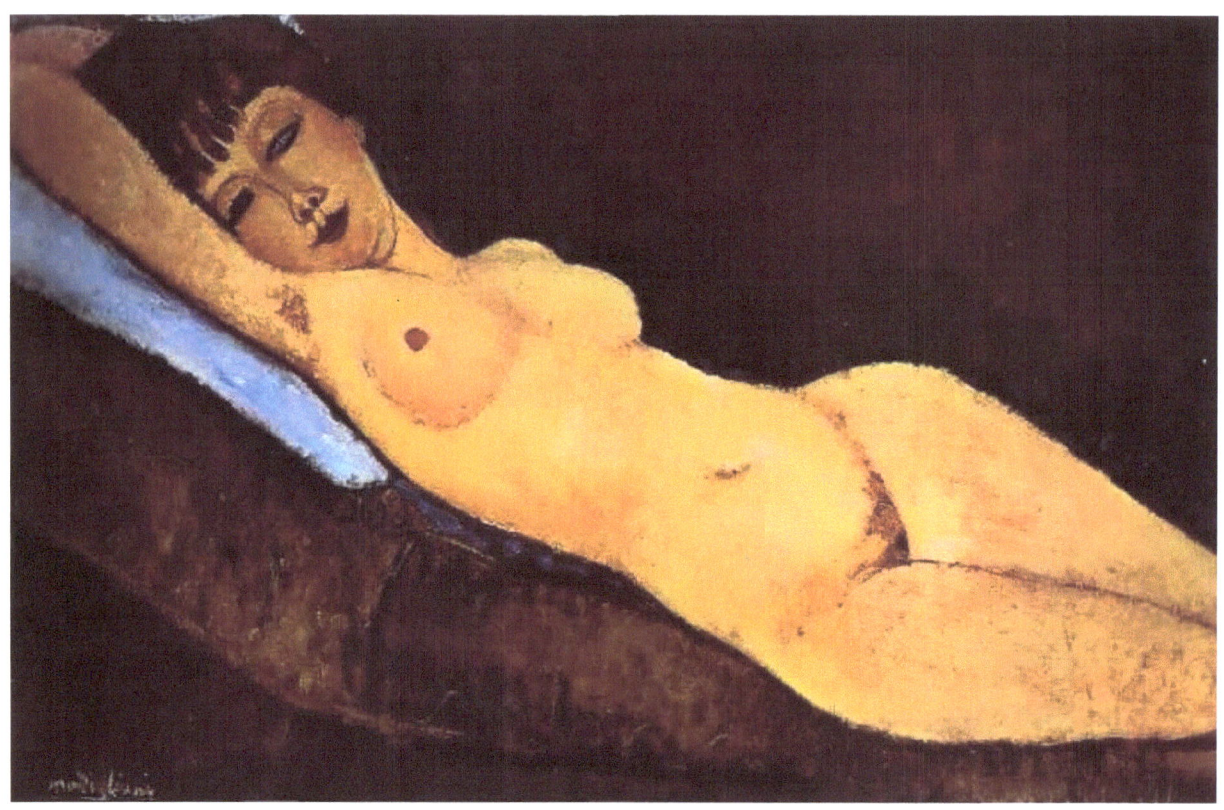

Reclining nude with Blue Cushion, 1917; Place of Creation: Paris, France

Expressionism; Collection of Nathan Cummings, New York, USA

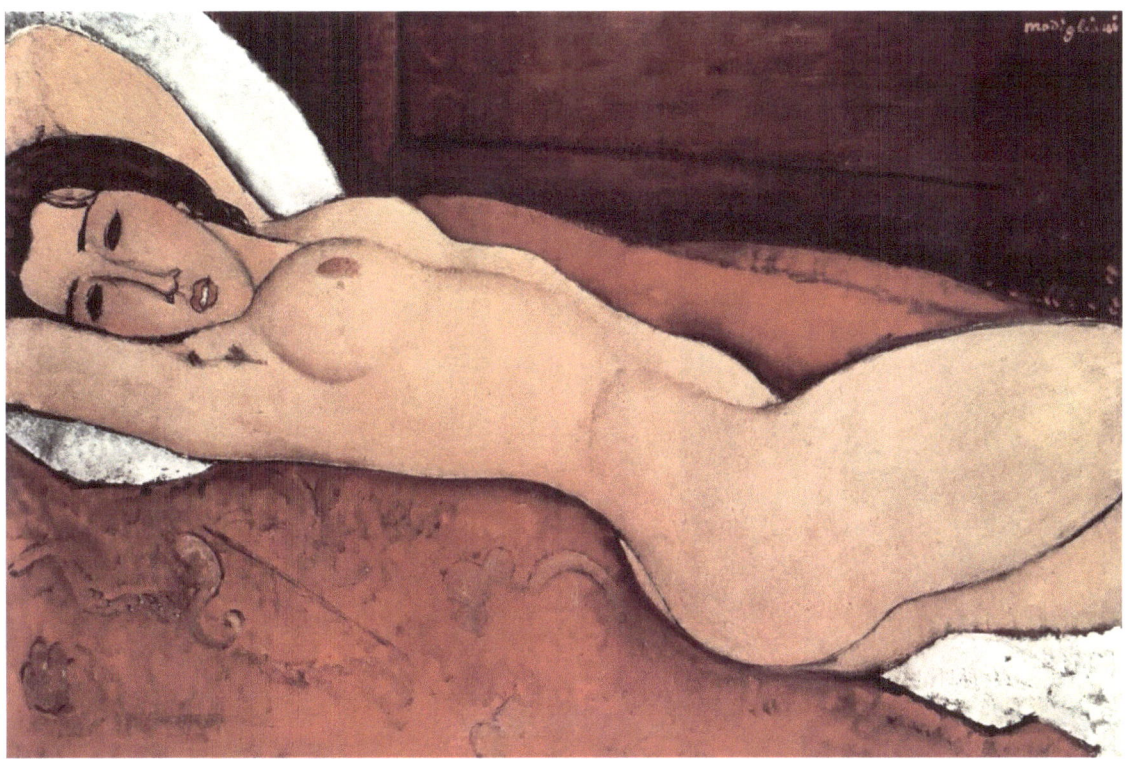

Reclining nude with folded arms behind her head, 1917; Paris, France; **Expressionism, Private Collection**

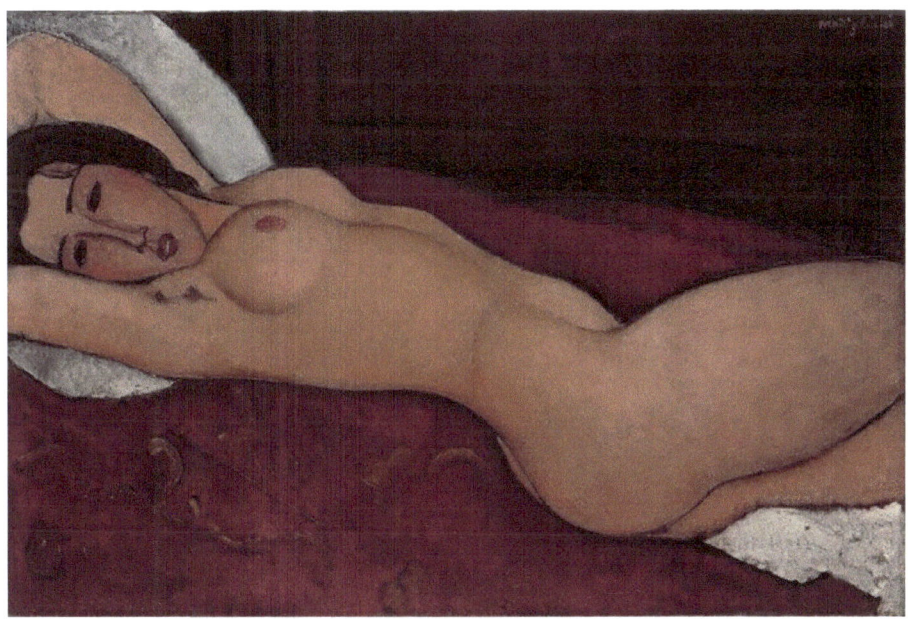

Reclining nude, 1917; Paris, France; Expressionism; Museum of Modern Art, New York, USA

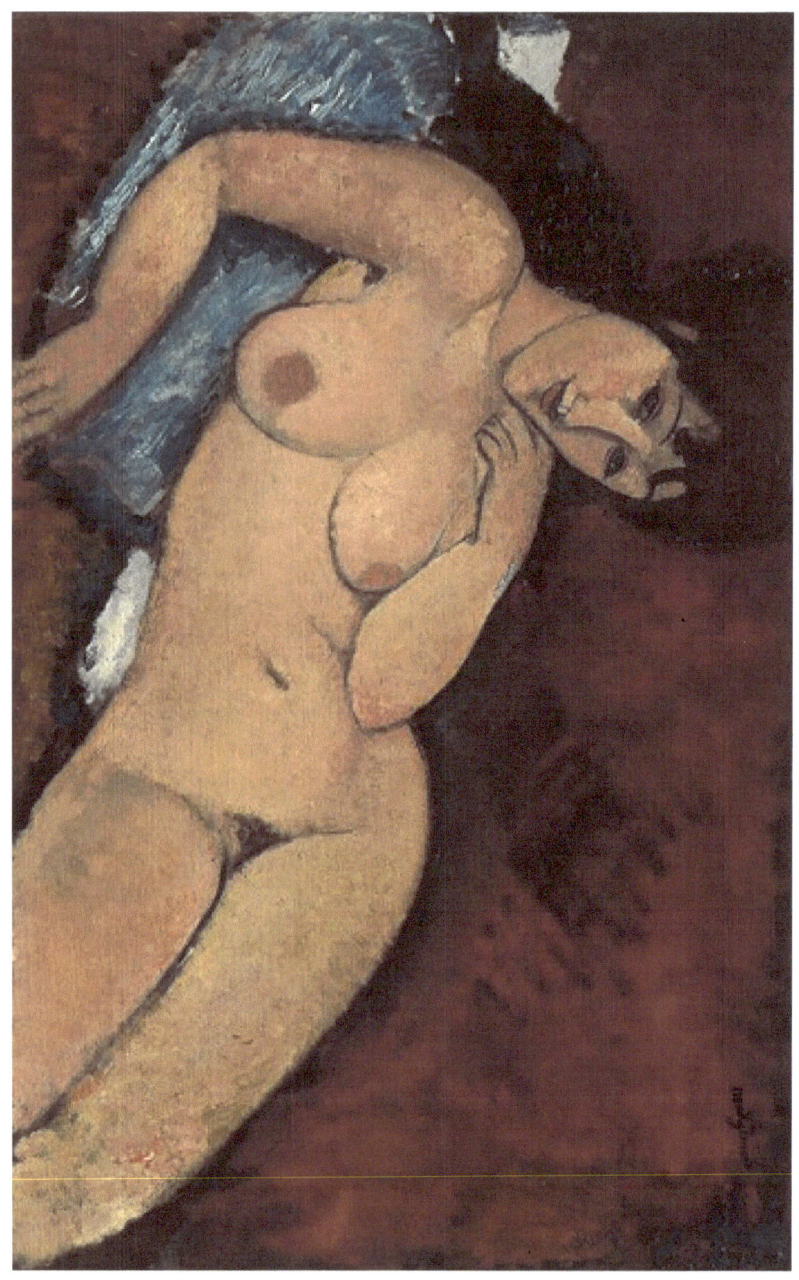

Nude on a Blue Cushion; Paris, France; Expressionism

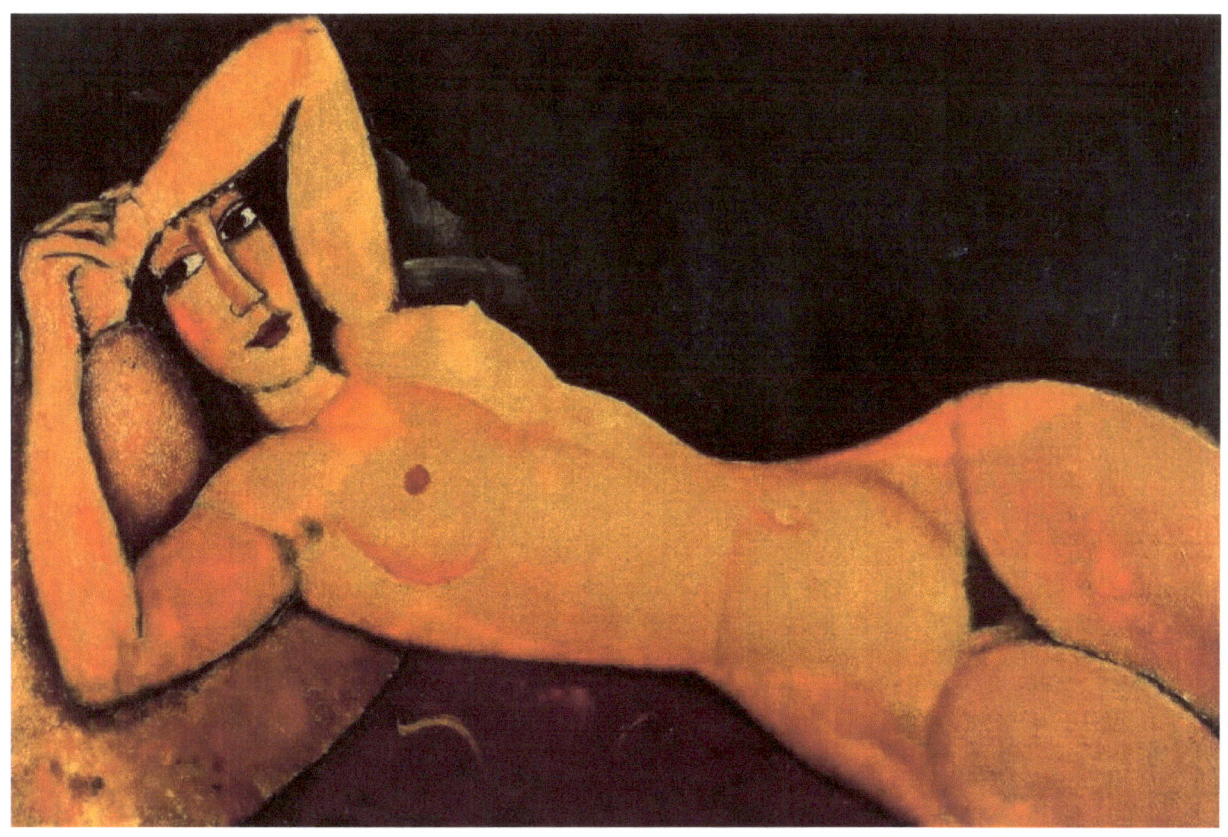

Reclining nude with Left Arm Resting on Forehead, 1917; Paris, France; **Expressionism, Private Collection**

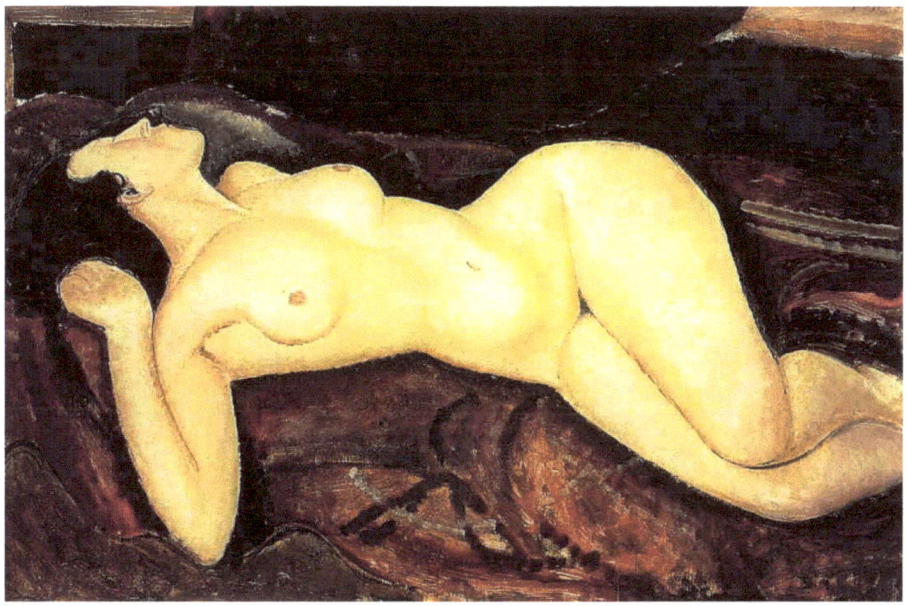

Recumbent nude, 1917; Paris, France; Expressionism; Private Collection

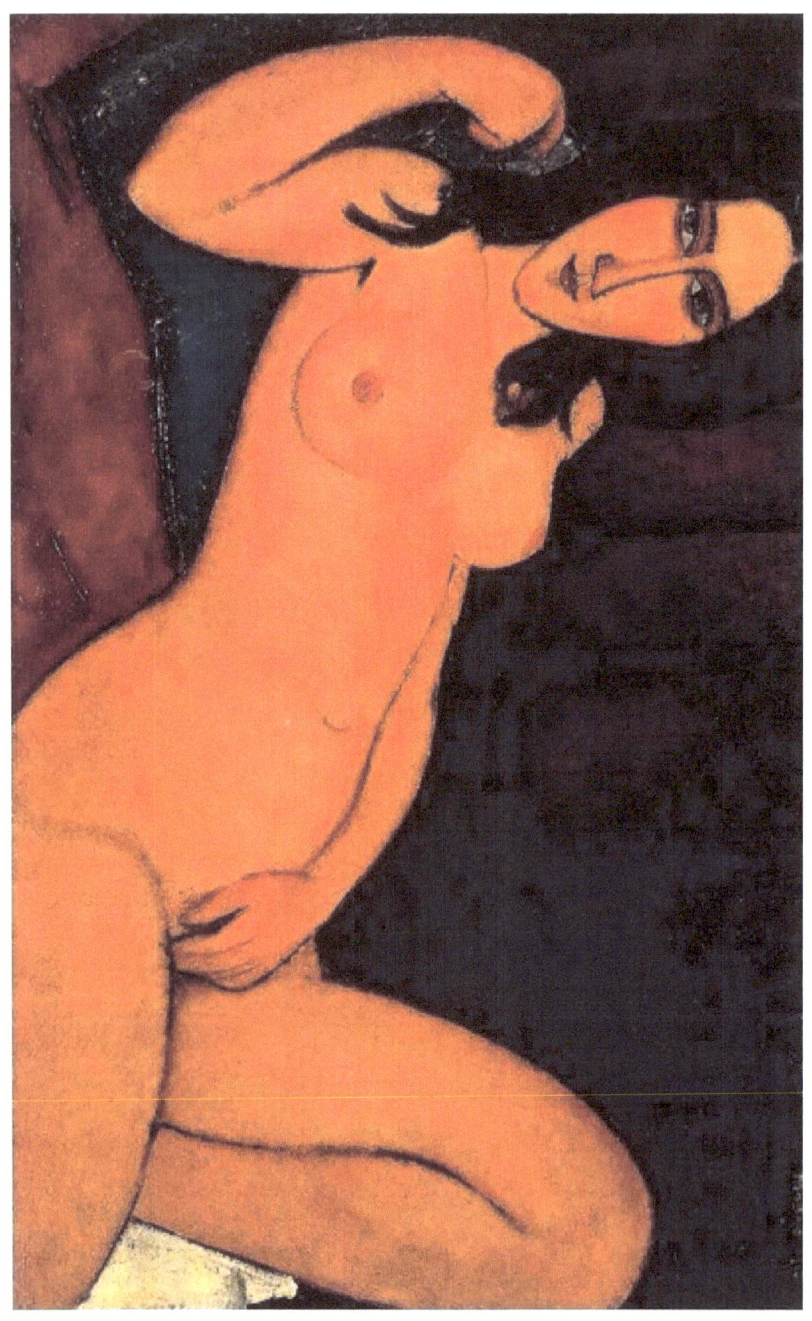

Reclining nude, 1917; Paris, France; Expressionism, Osaka City Museum of Modern Art, Japan

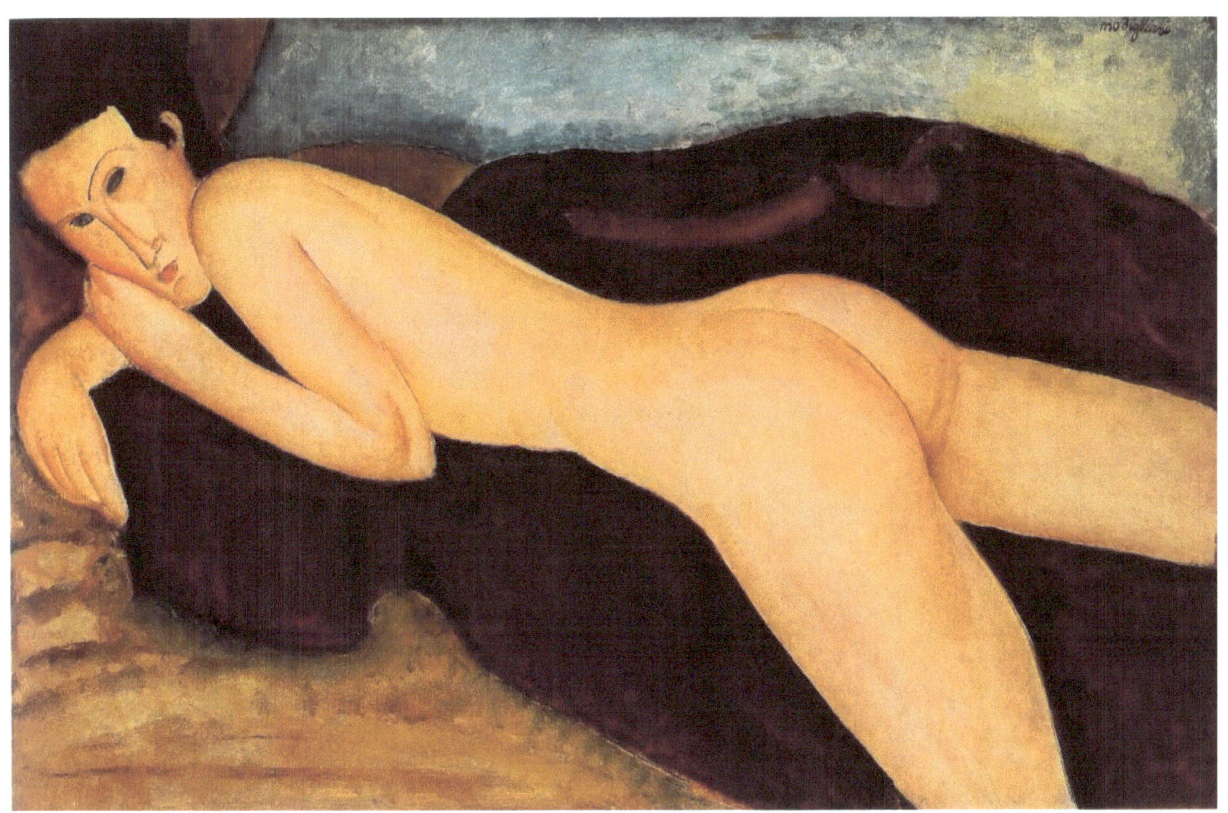

Reclining nude from the Back, 1917; Paris, France; **Expressionism**,

The Barnes Foundation, Merion, Pennsylvania, USA

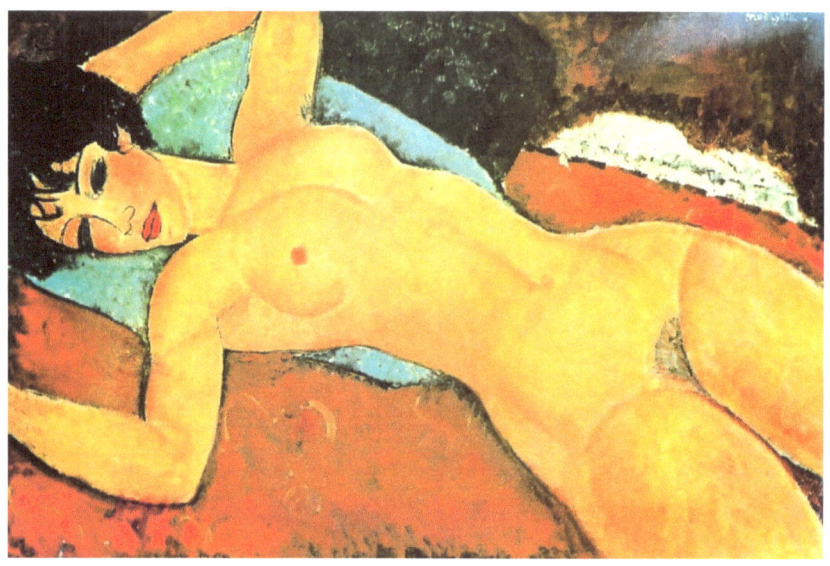

Sleeping Nude with Arms Open (Red Nude), 1917; Paris, France;
Expressionism

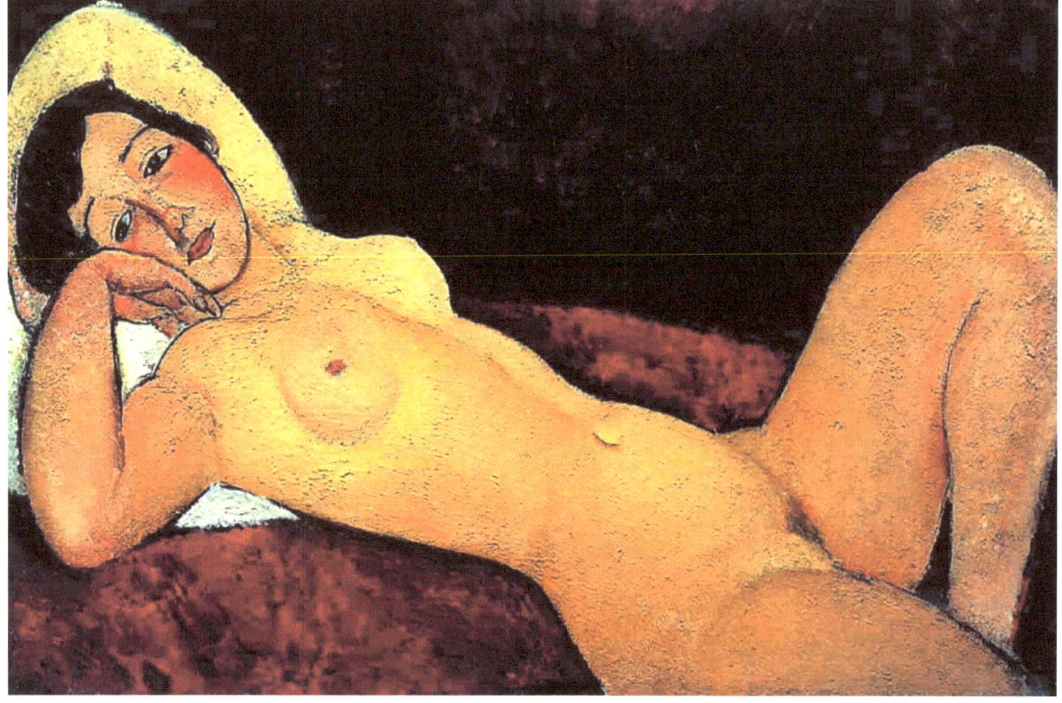

Reclining nude, 1917; Paris, France; Expressionism, Private Collection

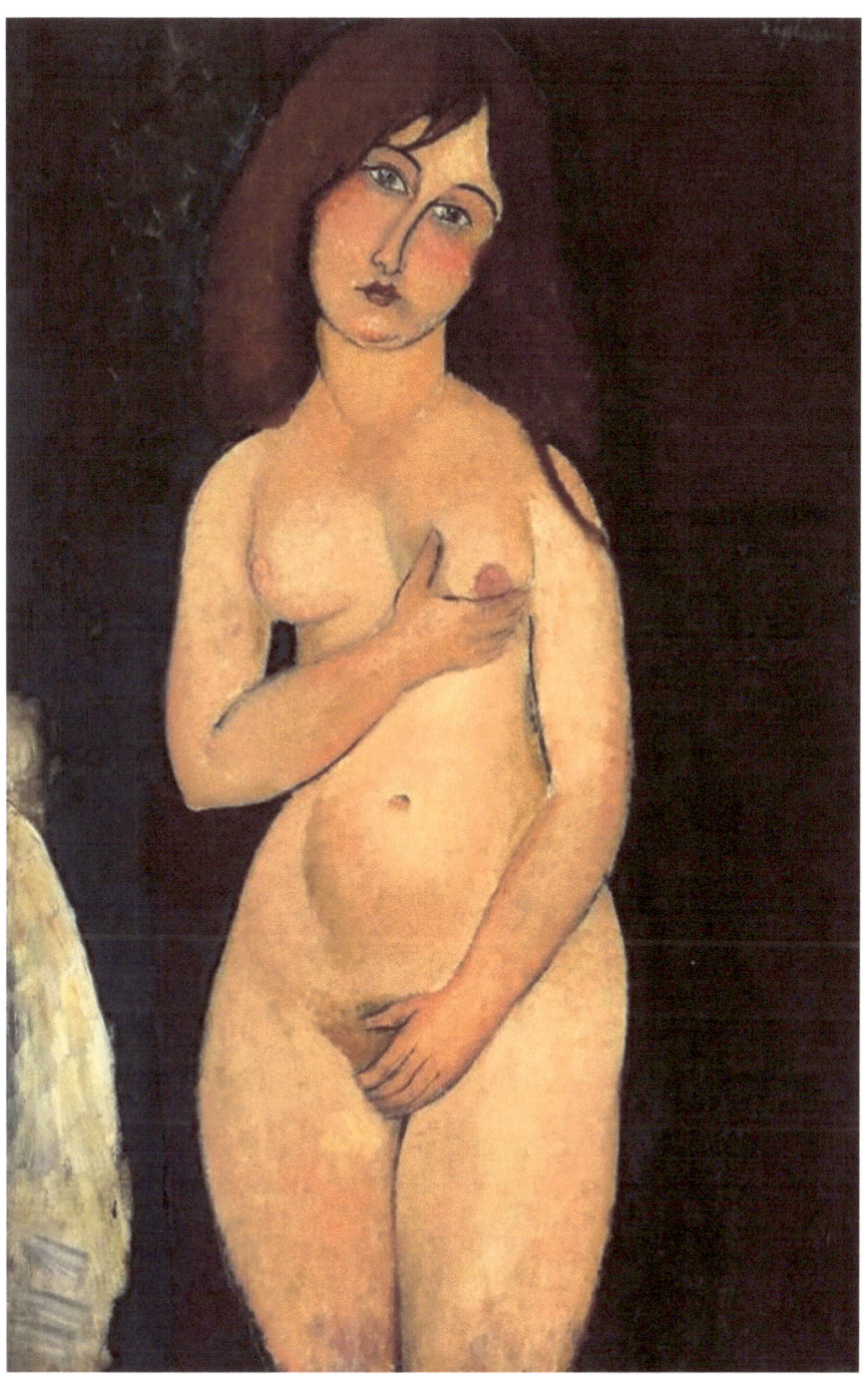

Venus (Standing nude), 1917; Paris, France; Expressionism, Private Collection

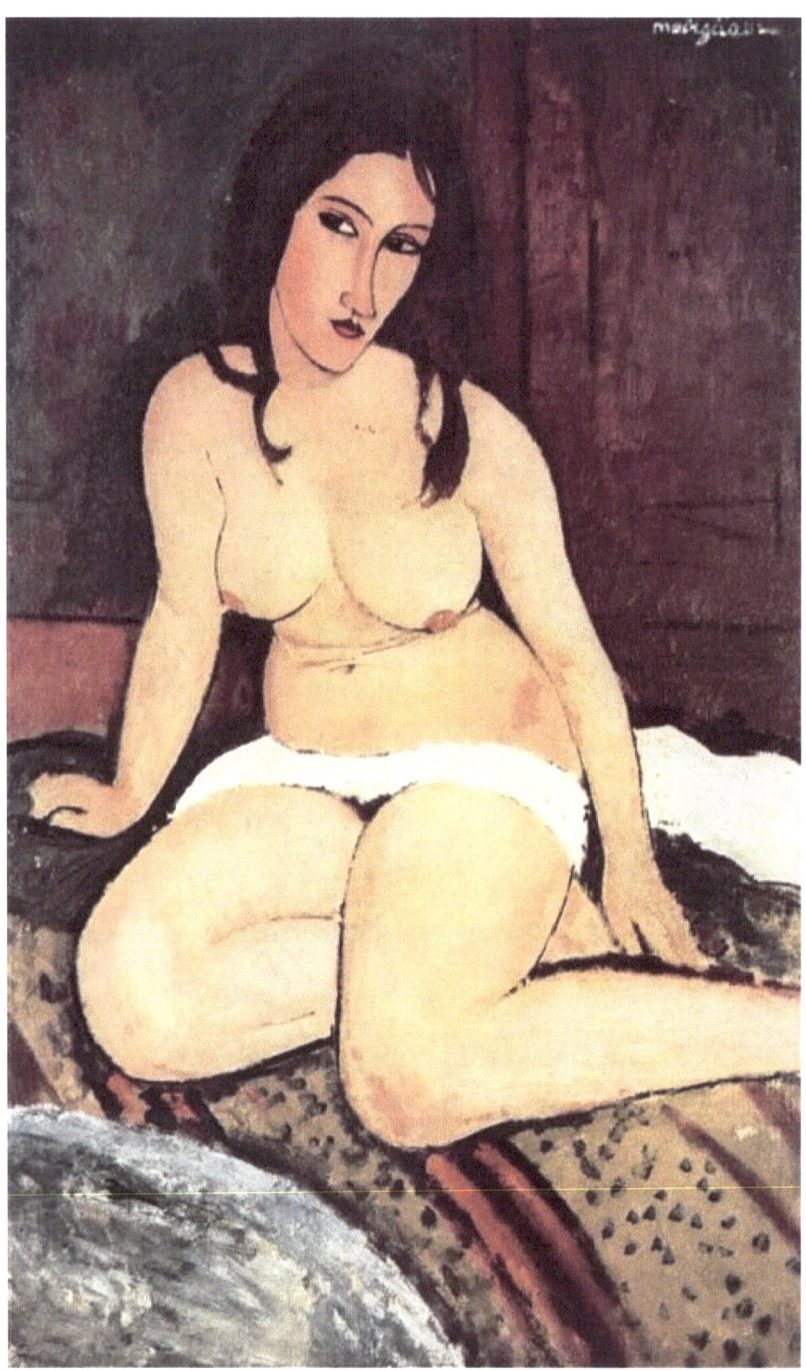

Seated Nude, **1917; Paris, France; Expressionism, Koninklijk Museum voor Schone Kunsten**

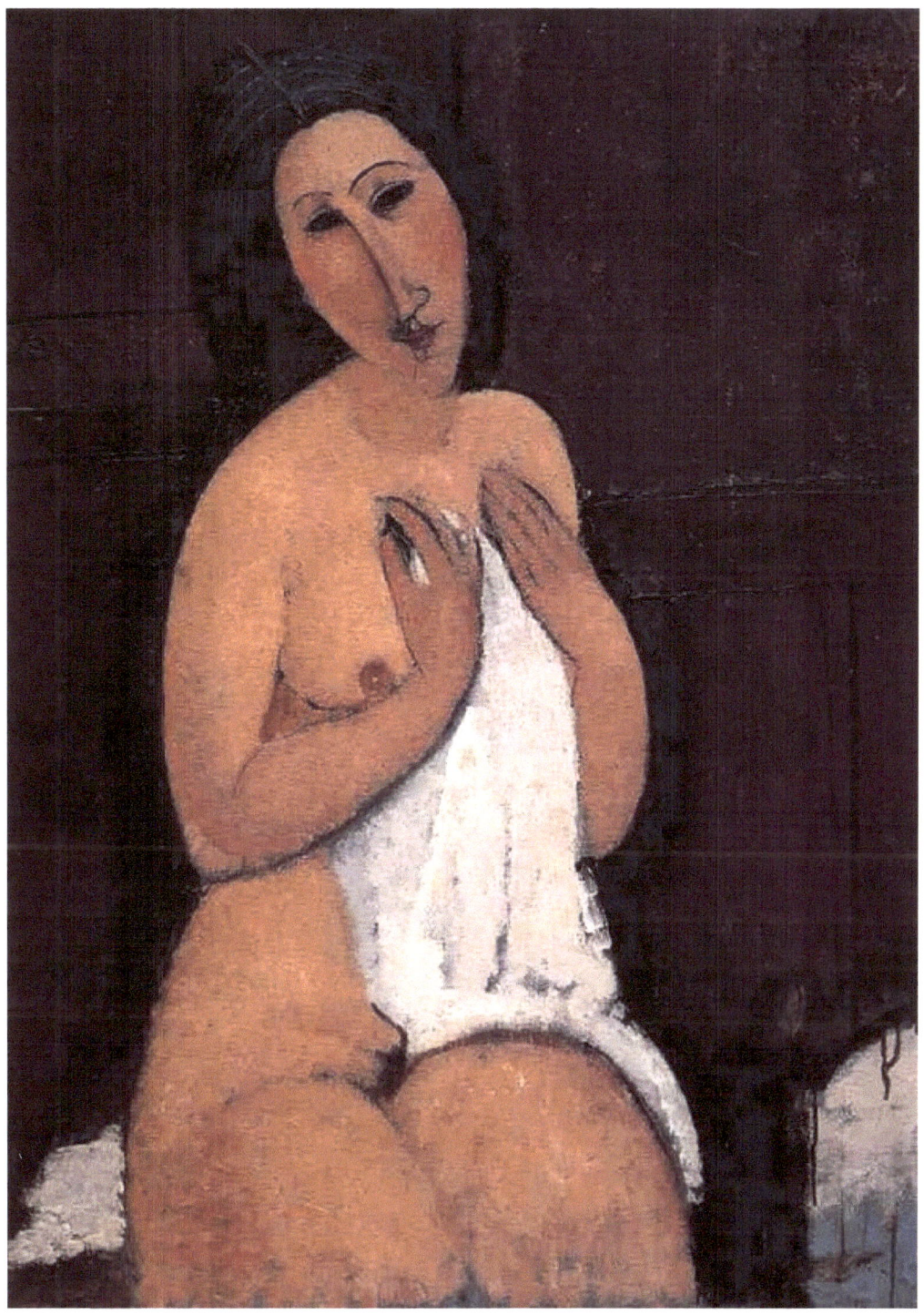

Seated nude with a Shirt, 1917; Paris, France; Expressionism;

Musée d'Art moderne, Lille, France

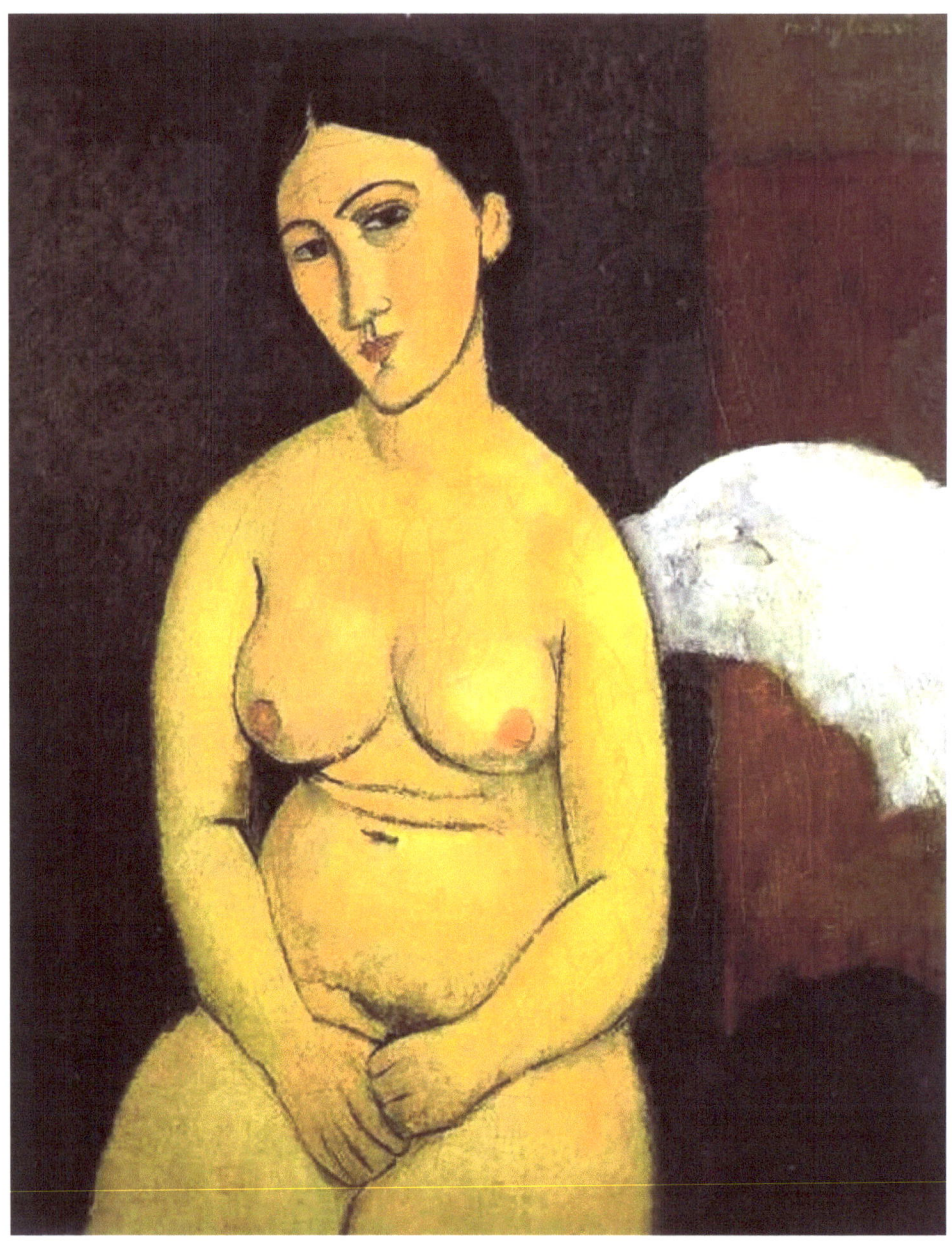

Seated nude, 1917; Paris, France; Expressionism, Private Collection

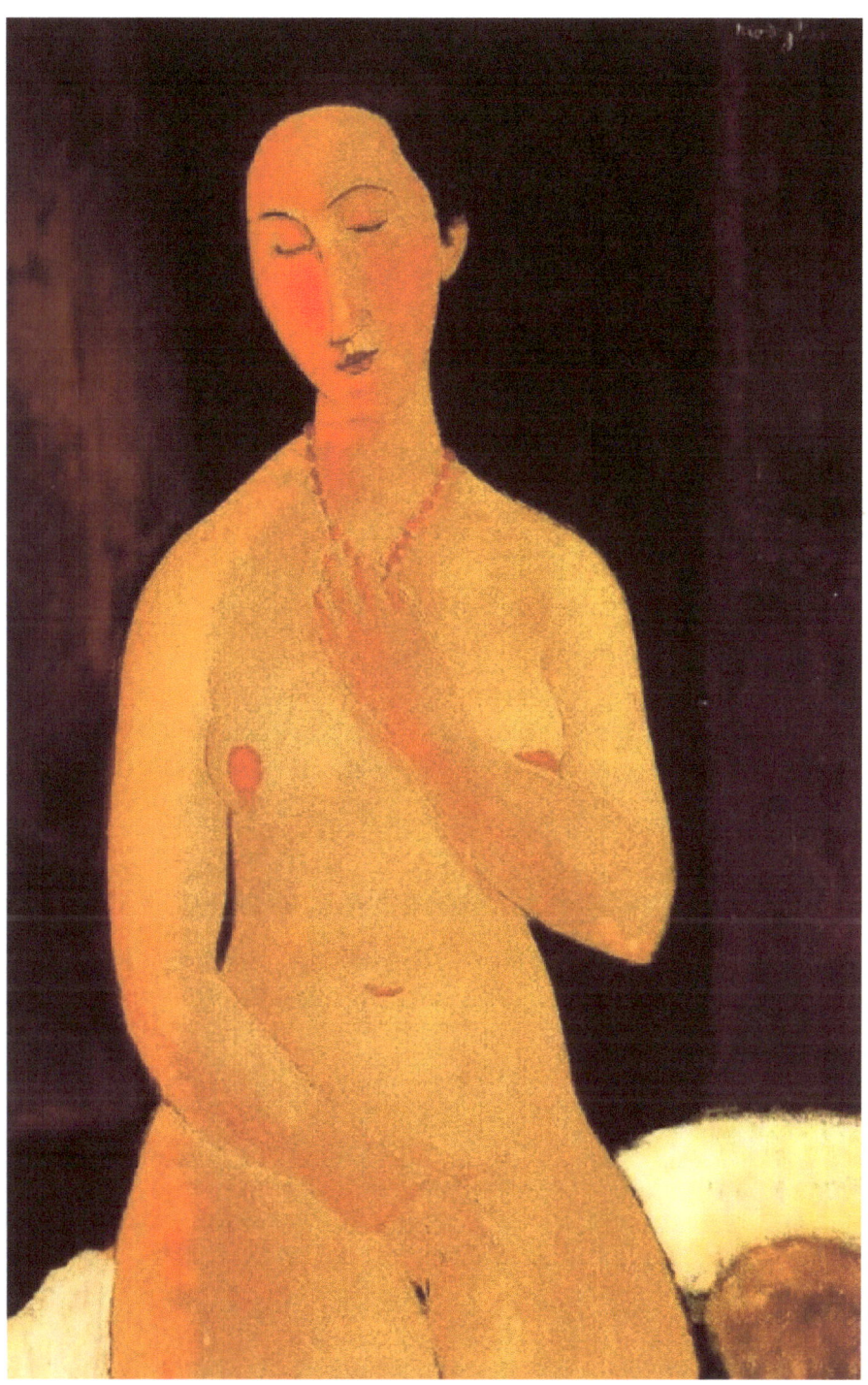

Seated nude with Necklace, 1917; Paris, France, Expressionism

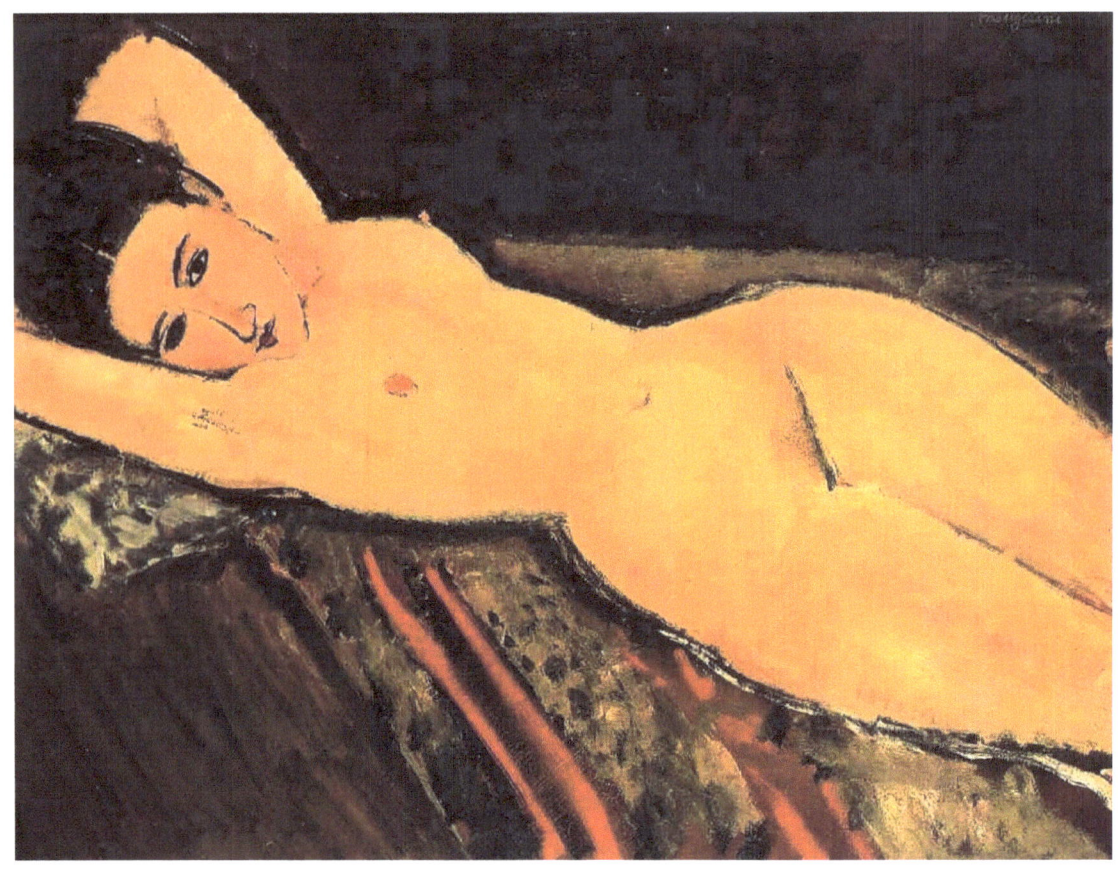

Reclining nude with Arms Folded under Her Head, 1916; Paris, France;

Expressionism, Bührle Foundation, Zürich, Switzerland

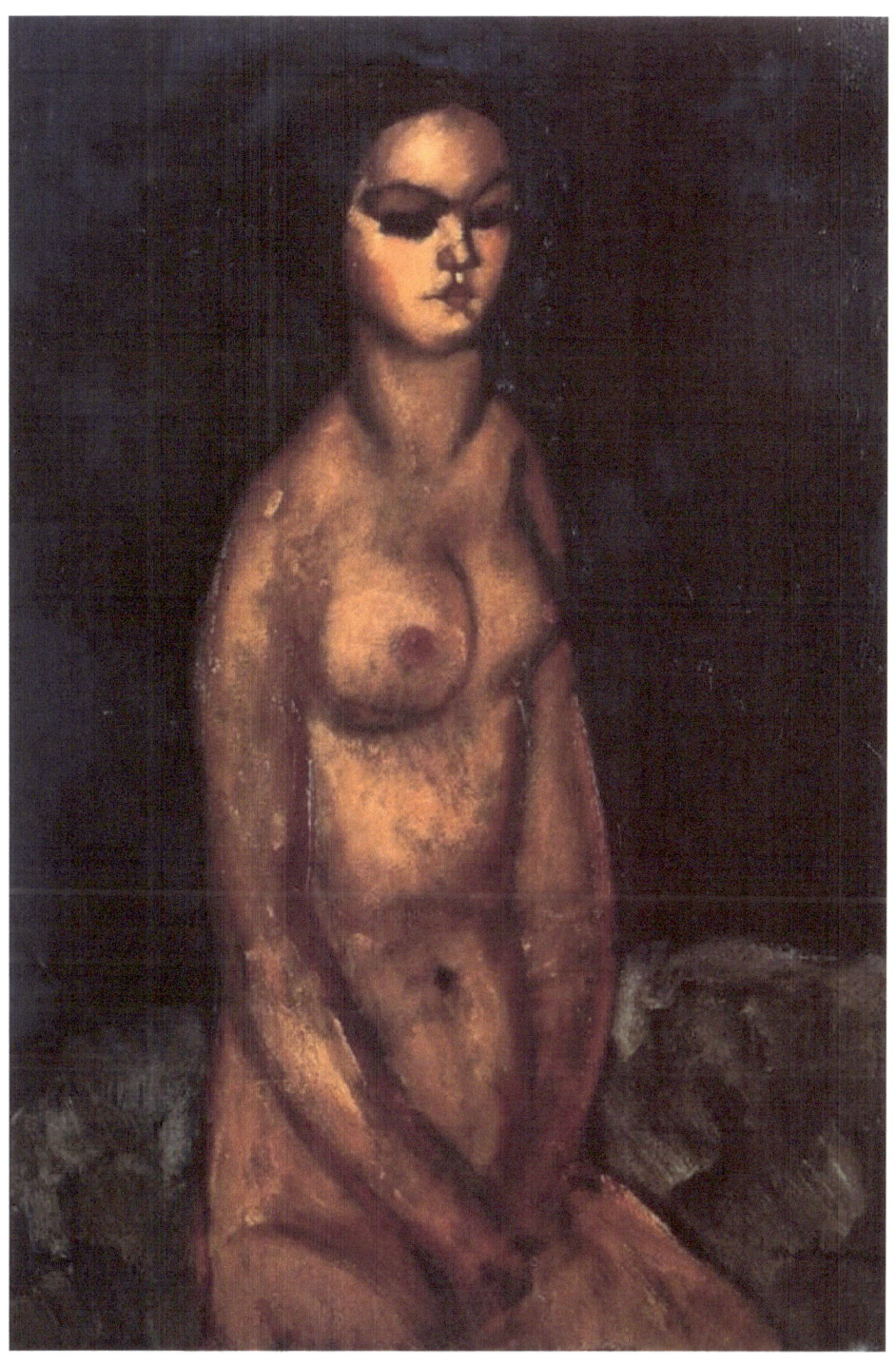

Seated nude, 1908, Paris, France; Expressionism, Private Collection

www.ingramcontent.com/pod-product-compliance
Lightning Source LLC
Chambersburg PA
CBHW050417180526
45159CB00005B/2306